WINNING AT GIN

CHESTER WANDER

with

CY RICE

Melvin Powers
Wilshire Book Company

12015 Sherman Road, No. Hollywood, CA 91605

ISBN 0-87980-351-7

Contents

This book is dedicated to
my wife Etta, always by my side,
to my sweet daughter, Karen,
to my son, Ricky,
to my mother, and
in fond memory of my father,
Fred Wander.—C.W.

Introduction

There are fifty million and one gin rummy players in the United States—the one being Chester Wander, International Gin Rummy Champion. In a game where almost anybody able to hold ten cards in his hand considers himself an expert, Chet has a champion's crown to prove he's a top banana.

Chet has all the assorted skills necessary to be a success. He is intelligent, shrewd, patient, intuitive, flexible, and he possesses a photographic memory. The way he puts it is, "I'm a percentage player." He says playing percentages is the way to win at gin rummy, and he's got me convinced. I've often played against him at our club, the Indian Wells Country Club in Palm Desert, California. Golf—not gin. When we play gin, I prefer to play with him, not against him.

There are almost as many schools of thought about gin rummy as there are players. Learning Chet Wander's style of play can be your springboard from run-of-the-mill to expert playing. Chet's approach to the game is so different from the average player's it may surprise you. But your happiest surprise will come when you put it to the test.

If you're a gin player who likes to "make the game a little interesting," this book can put jingling dividends in your pocket. If you're a player who thinks it's all a matter of luck you'll find out what a pigeon this kind of player can be against a player who knows the score. All I can say is, if you're *any* kind of gin player—or even if you're not but would like to be—this book has more to offer you than anything else you can read on the subject. You can't argue with success, and that is what Chet Wander has enjoyed in this popular indoor pastime for thirty years.

Incidentally, while you're mastering the game you'll have lots of laughs along the way, as Chet tells how he became champion and how being champion changed his life.

Gin rummy is a household word. If every player in the U.S.A. shuffled his cards at once, it would blow up such a storm that everybody would probably lock in for the winter—making sure they had a deck of cards on hand.

If you were fortunate enough to have Chet Wander around during the long winter months, you would emerge—when spring came around again—a real pro.

DESI ARNAZ

Las Vegas, Here I Come

1

Fate can deal you a winning hand in life, and if you pick it up and play your cards correctly, the dark clouds of failure drift away and the clear skies of the future show. Some claim your fate is dictated by the stars; others that it's an act of Providence. I'm not certain as to the cause, but I am as to the effect. I do know that a hypothetical wheel of fortune spun and stopped on my number to make an average guy into a celebrity overnight.

One of the most descriptive words in the English language is BROKE. The word has plenty of synonyms: impoverished, insolvent, and a rash of others. But they all have the same meaning: No money.

So why fancify my condition in 1958 with a multisyllabled word when the simplest of them baldly described my personal finances? I felt as though the entire weight of the world had fallen on my hip pocket—the one holding my wallet—crushing, pulverizing, burying me underneath. I was an ant under the Alps, without a shovel.

Now, one of the unwritten duties of a wife is to buoy her husband's sagging spirits, repair his ruptured ego—anything to remove his mind from troubles.

Mine tried by suggesting, "Let's play a few hands of gin."

There's hardly a gin rummy player of the approximately fifty million in the United States who, upon hearing this proposition, can resist saying—even in the midst of pestilence or famine—"Cut you for deal."

I won, and as I shuffled the cards my mind rambled. Here I was, the head of an interior decorating firm, furnishing tract homes scattered over southern California. Operating from Fuller-ton, we had built up about a hundred thousand dollars in equities. One of the key companies we dealt with had folded; then others followed in bankruptcies totaling nearly five million dollars. Our accounts were uncollectible. Personal debts were piling up. Prac-tically my sole remaining asset was my close resemblance to comedian Phil Silvers, but a scrupulously honest man couldn't cash in on that. And I considered myself an honest man.

I was forty-two years old, with a wife named Etta and a daughter, Karen, age five. The future of the Wander family was in grave jeopardy.

"Your play," Etta interrupted my thoughts.

I sorted my cards, arranged them, picked a card from the deck, and felt a tingling at the nape of my neck.

"Gin," I said, laying down my hand.

The next morning over breakfast—the menu dictated by the newly felt economic pinch (small eggs instead of jumbo, Pream instead of cream, margarine instead of butter)—Etta announced:

"I want you to enter the tournament."

I shook my head. "You know I'm getting too old to play tennis. I . . ."

"Not tennis," she corrected, "gin. Gin rummy. The tournament in Las Vegas. First prize is ten thousand dollars. Entries include Hawaii, Mexico, Canada . . ."

"Why, that's international!"

"So what? You used to live in Brooklyn, didn't you?"

"But . . ."

"No buts. You're the greatest player in the world."

"On what do you base that conclusion?" I asked.

"You can beat me," Etta said.

I didn't laugh. My wife is one hell of a player.

Once the germ of the idea was planted, interest gradually mounted. Obstacles loomed: travel expenses, hotel, food, an entry fee of a hundred dollars, not to mention hundreds of formidable opponents.

Etta had a solution.

"We'll pawn my wedding ring."

I protested. "That ring is your most valuable possession."

"No. You are."

Her faith was touching. I had never played in a tournament.

Normally I only went in for social games. Together with seven other married couples in Fullerton, we met weekly, playing for a nominal amount. Basically I didn't play to gamble—more for relaxation, to relieve my mind of problems—although a few times I sat down for fairly high stakes.

I usually won.

Throughout a period of many years I had assimilated the game, digesting it slowly and thoroughly, trying to analyze and learn from every mistake that cropped up. I had progressed, I believed, to a skill plateau where I was unafraid to contest anyone.

I thought, why not take a fling at it. I'm broke anyway, so what have I got to lose?

I kidded, "I wonder if the hotel in Las Vegas will give us a room without you wearing a wedding ring."

She said, "We'll soon find out."

She got up, went to the garage, and I heard the sound of the car pulling out. About an hour later she returned. The ring was missing from her finger.

She handed me five one hundred dollar bills.

That evening friends dropped in, and when we apprised them of our decision, there was collective headshaking. "You're crazy," they declared, asking, "Don't you realize the odds against you?" and answering before I could, "They're astronomical. Those sharpies know what the card is almost before they pick it up."

"And my husband knows the card before it's dealt," countered Etta, with more loyalty than logic.

If we were to journey to Las Vegas in a style commensurate with our bankroll, a covered wagon would have been in order. Not good enough for members of the Wander family. My credo is if you're about to go down the drain, go down in style. Had Etta and I been passengers on the ill-fated Titanic, knowing every space on the lifeboats was filled, we would have sat on the tilting deck in all our finery—Etta bedecked with jewelry and me writing out checks for every last cent I had in the bank and tossing them into the wind. That's my idea of a triumphal exit.

Off to the Los Angeles International Airport went the three Wanders to enplane on the great adventure. There was never any debate about whether Karen should come along. Our idea of family is that, fair weather or foul, we're all in it together, and as long as we stick together we'll come out all right. Stormy weather delayed the takeoff. Waiting for the rain to blow away, I played a few games of gin with Etta, not only as a time killer but as a conditioner.

Let me stress right here that training and conditioning are as important in gin as they are to a track athlete with his eye on the gold medal in the 400 meter run at the Olympic games. To prepare for a gin rummy tournament, at least two solid weeks of continuous play against first class opposition is a must. Technique, patience, self-discipline, concentration—all of these have to be honed to a fine edge so you'll be able to play shifting patterns when it counts. The edge comes in knowing how to play percentages. Play percentages in any game through life and you'll finish in the win column. Percentage is the foundation Las Vegas is built on.

The mind must be whipped, flayed, and chastised—acts of recklessness are unpardonable; and with it the ego has to be kept under lock and key. If you make a brilliant play, don't let your ego swell up like a balloon. A balloon is easily punctured. If you make a stupid play, forget it in a hurry. In gin the action is rapid, and once a play has been made you can't afford either to cry over spilt milk or get heady over your own shrewdness. You have to keep yourself alert to what's coming, because this is a game where one move can change the complexion of a hand completely.

One thing I had to stamp indelibly on my mind: in a tournament I would be playing solely against a score. The knock becomes the chief factor here.

If I may digress a moment from the tournament, I want to hammer home an important basic rule of gin rummy: MOST HANDS SHOULD BE PLAYED TO KNOCK.

For those of you who are beginners, let me explain what "knock" means. It's a word that will appear dozens of times in the following pages; it's the number one word in the gin rummy player's lexicon; it's the aim of the game.

At the start of a gin rummy game, each player is dealt ten cards, and the next card is turned face-up on the table. The goal is to achieve a hand which falls into groups of three or more cards either of the same face value or in uninterrupted sequence of the same suit. If all ten cards are used in such combinations, the player can go gin. However, a player can end the game before this point, as long as the face value of the unmatched cards in his hand does not total more than the value of the turned-up card on the table. To end the game in this way is to knock, and naturally this situation will come up many more times than the opportunity to go gin. The only time a game *must* end in gin is when the turned-up card is an ace.

Unfortunately, most players are tempted to hold out in almost every game until they can go gin, bypassing chance after chance to knock. This is the worst mistake a gin rummy player can make. That's why I have selected this as the first rule to give you, and it's not too soon to repeat it: MOST HANDS SHOULD BE PLAYED TO KNOCK.

The name of the game is gin, but that doesn't mean you play for gin with every hand. Not even with most of them. Each hand should be played according to how it sets up and develops, but in the majority of instances this will mean that you should knock at the earliest possible opportunity. It's no coincidence that the most frequently heard wail among gin players is, "I shoulda knocked!"

Memorize that rule well. If you do, I can assure you more of those nickels or quarters will come your way than the other guy's in your regular Thursday night game. Once you've committed this rule to the gin rummy computer in your head, *then* learn when to use it and when not to. Naturally, when an ace is the turn-up card, you have no choice but to go for gin. But say your knock is three. Chances are your gin opportunities will form just as easily, or almost as easily, as your knock opportunities. So will the other fellow's. This kind of situation calls for shrewd judgment and alertness on your part in setting up and playing your hand.

But let's take another situation: You and I are playing and you can knock with ten, while I still have twenty points in my hand. You go two or three more picks and you don't improve your hand; the chances at that point are against your improving it. In the meantime, I'm picking up a steady advantage. While you're still debating whether to get out, I knock with six. You could have picked up ten points from me; instead, I beat you for four.

Or it may be that I'm sitting there with a hand that needs one card to make it jell. While you're using up valuable plays trying to improve your hand by a few points, I may pull the card I need out of the deck—or even pick it up from one of your discards— and gin.

You can label that one of the biggest mistakes the average gin player makes. If you knock as soon as you can—even if the game has progressed three-quarters of the way down the deck—the percentages are in your favor, everything else being equal, to win the hand.

If you can just forget the name of the game—gin—and play the game as it should be played, most of the time you'll be playing "knock rummy." If you have a knocking point of ten or nine, two melds will often enable you to knock. If the knock is five, you're going to need at least a three-card and a four-card meld in your hand to be under the call.

However, if you're playing someone who's familiar with your game, that factor may at times call for different strategy.

"Gin."

"Huh?"

"Gin. You're not paying attention, darling." It was Etta. We were still at the airport, and while my mind was wandering she had just won a big hand from me. Which just goes to prove my point: If you're playing someone who knows your game, you especially have to be on your toes every minute.

I suddenly awakened to another fact. Our plane was still not ready to take off, and the deadline for registering in the Las Vegas Tournament was only a few hours away. How do you explain to airline officials that it's urgent for you to keep a date with a gin rummy game?

Finally, after another grueling hour's wait, we were airborne pointed in the direction of Las Vegas.

Arriving at the gambling capital of the world. we checked in at the Tropicana Hotel, then rushed to the Sands Hotel to register at the Tournament headquarters. Play was scheduled to be held at eight major hotels which had joined forces to sponsor the Tournament, all members of the Las Vegas Charities Foundation.

"You're lucky," the man at the desk told me upon receiving my one hundred dollar entry fee.

"Not yet," I said cautiously.

"What I mean," he explained, "is that the entries were supposed to close at ten this morning but we postponed the deadline an hour."

I glanced at my watch. It was one minute to eleven. I was just under the wire.

That night we visited several of the sites of play, and I met some of the other entrants. I didn't learn much through observation. They were tall, short, fat, skinny. One wore a monocle. I wondered if it would fall out if his opponent went gin on the first few picks.

One man looked as big and strong as a wrestler. Fortunately, in gin rummy a Herculean opponent needn't intimidate you. He may be the number one weight lifter in the world, but a few quick knocks and an undercut will cut him down to size. Perhaps his hands resemble hams and can ball into ominous fists, yet the cards he deals you are the same standard size as those you deal him. It's what's inisde the skull that counts, and if he has a gargantuan one, that doesn't mean he'll memorize his cards better. It might mean there's more vacant space for a little deuce of hearts to become lost in. At least you can hope so.

One entrant was from the Army. His uniform bore a sergeant's stripes. He was the barracks champ, and his buddies had pooled their money to send him to the Tournament. Well, I thought, those stripes might frighten some of the boys back at the post, but here they wouldn't make any difference.

He got his brains beat out in the first round.

Women were also entered. This was one time when you could battle the other sex with no fear of fingernails. If you play with the average woman—and should you call any woman "average," you'd better grab your hat and run—she generally throws science out the window, playing strictly on hunches. She may hold two Kings, two Queens, two Jacks, two 10's, and if she has an Ace she'll throw it. And probably beat you.

But not in the long run.

Harry Ritz of the Ritz Brothers comedy team (he's the one in the middle who rolls his eyes) tells a story about playing gin with a woman. He was on a blind date, and when he arrived at her apartment the lights were so low he thought maybe Edison should try again. It was impossible to see her face.

She said, "Let's play some gin."

Harry inquired about the stakes.

She answered, "We'll play one game of two hundred points. If you beat me, you get a kiss."

"Suppose I blitz you?" Harry asked, always the man to look for an angle.

"Well . . ." she hesitated, her voice soft, "let's just say that you get an extra bonus."

Harry played like an inspired demon with the extra bonus dividend as an incentive. He was ahead on the score pad 178 to 0, needing only a 4 of clubs for gin and a blitz. This was precisely what she discarded, but before Harry could snatch it up she asked for a light for her cigarette.

He held the flickering torch in front of her face, and what was revealed caused him to recoil in horror. He let the 4 of clubs stay on the table, drew another card, and lost every hand they played after that.

"Sometimes it pays to lose," he commented later to one of his brothers.

If I had to compare gin rummy with any other game, I would say it's related to chess in the concentration it requires, although faster decisions are involved in gin. Powerful concentration is an essential factor and can provide the player who has it with a distinct advantage. Mathematics are my forte and I like to sit down and figure out what I've got and what you've got, running it through a comptometer-of-mind that tells me how I can get what I need from you.

Then it becomes a question of strategy, just as in chess.

That night before retiring I read the official playing rules of the Tournament. Changes were to occur in the future.

1. Head-to-head play (two players only).
2. Cut for deal for each new game. Low card starts first deal and keeps score. Ace low.
3. Games will be for 125 points the first two sessions. (NO Hollywood method of scoring, which is progressive type, or three games across.)
4. Losers shuffle cards after every deal, opponent cuts, and loser continues game by dealing.
5. Style of play will be Oklahoma Gin:
   (a) Players are dealt ten cards each.
   (b) The twenty-first card will be turned up, and will denote the number of points with which each player is permitted to knock. If Ace appears, the hand is for gin.
   (c) The player who undercuts, or goes gin, will receive a twenty-five point bonus, plus the amount of points won.
6. Boxes are not counted for gin or undercut.

7. NO bonus for "Schneider" ("Blitz")
8. NO new deals by agreement or "Frischers."
9. In the event a card is seen or exposed, to which a player is not entitled, the card is to be openly shown, placed back in the stack and shuffled, with the same hand continuing.
10. Spades will not be double, nor any other suit.
11. The player who draws the fiftieth card may terminate the hand by knocking or calling gin. If he discards, his opponent may pick this card for knocking or gin rummy ONLY. If this card is not used, the hand is terminated.
12. Rank of cards: King (high), Queen, Jack, Ten, Nine, Eight, Seven, Six, Five, Four, Three, Two, Ace. (NO Ace-King-Queen sequences permitted.)
13. Value of cards: Picture cards ten (10) each, Ace is one (1), others face value. Fifty-two cards in deck.
14. All finalists must play twenty games.
15. All participants play opponents only once.

The program book for the Tournament went on to explain that finalists would be determined on the basis of the best top sixteen won and lost percentages. In case of ties, there would be a straight knockout (dead heat) game of 150 points between the tied players.

In the finals, the first round would consist of 300 points, the second round 350 points, the semifinals 400 points, and the final round 500 points.

Finished reading the rules, I turned toward Etta. "Do you know what a Frischer is?" In my many years of playing gin rummy I had picked up many colorful expressions used by players in different parts of the country. I knew, for instance, that "Schneider" or "Blitz" meant holding your opponent scoreless for an entire game. But "Frischer" was a new one to me. Etta wasn't familiar with it either. "It must be a term they use in tournaments," she said. "If it's important, you'll find out."

Before turning out the lights, I asked Etta, "Any final instructions?"

"Yes. Don't drum on the table with your fingers when you have a good hand."

She was dead right about this mannerism of mine. It was a sure giveaway. I'd observed many idiosyncracies in other players that tipped off their strengths or weaknesses. Some players adjust their glasses, run hands through hair, others keep changing cards from one hand to the other. A close friend of mine pants heavily as his hand begins to shape up.

Superstitions are legion among gin devotees. I saw a man insist—after first learning the direction of the wind from a weather vane—on sitting with the wind at his back. Another always lays a two-headed penny on the table beside him. He'd do better to absorb some rudiments of the game inside the one head that God gave him.

I never had any superstitions. What is to happen will happen, has always been my motto, and I don't believe fetishes, charms, talismans, or amulets are going to help you to win in a card game. Etta and I have always subscribed to this line of thinking and followed it unswervingly, with no deviations.

Except in this International Tournament.

Suddenly we both were conscripted into the ranks of the superstitious millions. Etta said that as long as I kept winning she would continue wearing her lucky brown suit. I said I would also wear the same clothes I started with: a red sweater and crimson slacks.

I sometimes wonder whether my choice of clothes may have given me a slight psychological advantage, as red can be a disturbing color.

I yawned and reached for the light switch. My hand paused as I related, "I heard a funny one today. Someone asked, 'How many gin rummy players are there in the Tournament?' The answer was 'One out of ten.' "

Etta gave my shoulder a reassuring pat. "Wrong," she said, "one out of five hundred."

I knew who she meant.

The next morning my powers of concentration received a stern test. When we were on the way to breakfast, the door of an adjacent room opened and Jayne Mansfield emerged. For not more than a split second I glanced at her face and then away. I had not broken training.

The action started, and the contestants faced each other over cocktail tables on the stages in the main dining rooms of hotels that staged the big nightly shows. The ranks of contestants had swelled to five hundred and forty when play officially commenced. Among them were eighty-seven determined women. For once their ages and weights were unimportant.

To the disappointment of hundreds, kibitzers were banned from standing in back of the players' chairs. They were kept at a respectable distance, watching a scoreboard, and none could drop his pearls of wisdom into the ears of contestants. They kept their seats for six hours the first day, surviving with difficulty each game, straining forward in their seats in a fruitless attempt to see the hands. All in all, the kibitzing crowd underwent the largest mass frustration in the history of card playing.

Win or lose in this tourney, I was pleased to learn that around $25,000 of the proceeds was going to charity—including such worthy causes as the City of Hope, March of Dimes, the Heart Fund, etc.

The Tournament rules called for playing ten games a day for two successive days in order to qualify. I was assigned to the group that played at the Riviera Hotel. I got off to a slow 6-4 start. One of my victories was over a squirming gentleman, the only person I've ever seen do a Watusi without leaving his chair. This didn't bother me as long as the cards held still.

By nightfall I was mad. "I played too wild today," I said.

Etta was far from downhearted. She radiated confidence, despite the fact that her hands were sore and blistered from pulling the handles of slot machines. She had a hundred dollar jackpot to show for her wounds.

"What about tomorrow?" she asked.

"What do you mean, tomorrow?" I countered, my hackles rising. "I'll play safer, naturally. I let myself be influenced by the fact that we're playing 125 point games and I threw some of my principles out the window. You can be sure I won't make the same mistake twice."

"Then there's no cause to worry," Etta concluded.

Well, the next day would tell the tale.

A point in my favor was that I wouldn't have any trouble sleeping as some of my friends do after a session. I don't bring lost hands to bed with me. Many wives report husbands mumbling during the night, "I knock . . . I knock with two . . . I should've taken the card," and tossing and turning in bed until dawn.

A builder acquaintance of mine, when asked by his wife to help her select wallpaper for the bedroom, replied, "Get the cheapest and blankest you can find." When questioned why, he answered, "My gin hands are going to appear on it every night anyway, and I don't want any fancy patterns in the way when I replay them."

As Tournament play resumed, I felt in top form. On the second day I won nine matches against only one loss, giving me an over-all record of fifteen wins out of twenty.

Would this be enough to get me into the finals? I knew it would be close. Only the sixteen players with the best won and lost percentage would become finalists. I listened as the names of the finalists were called out. I glanced over at Etta. She was still wearing her lucky brown suit. The tenth name was announced, with a 16-to-4 win record. After a pause, the official declared that all players with 15-to-5 records would compete for the remaining six spots in sudden death matches of 150 points.

Since the semifinals were scheduled to begin the next morning, the tie-breaking games had to be played that same night. Fourteen tired players reported to a banquet room at the Sands for the tie-breaking games which started about eight o'clock at night. I understand there was an additional player with 15-to-5 who, for reasons I have never learned, did not show up. Possibly he threw in the towel too soon by not waiting to find out if fifteen wins would make the grade.

I won one of the six open finalist spots in the play that night. Another of the spots was won by Bert Shubin, a realtor from Edmonton, Alberta, Canada, whom I was to see again in the final match. The next day I breezed along to reach the semifinals. The other three survivors were José Lassman, a Mexico City sweater manufacturer; Ronald Sleater, Salt Lake City businessman; and Bert Shubin.

The semis and finals were covered by closed circuit television cameras. The audience followed each card player on large TV screens. This acted as a slight healing balm to the kibitzers, but they still fidgeted and whispered excitedly among themselves, casting longing glances at the area directly behind the players' chairs.

Veteran gin enthusiasts called my contest with José Lassman the most exciting game of the entire Tournament. Lassman was a strong favorite to win the tournament. Earlier in the day he had eliminated Hank Greenspun, editor of the *Las Vegas Sun,* another favorite. I was considered an underdog.

Toward the end of my game with Lassman, when we were both

within twenty-five points to victory, I heard a loud cry from the audience watching play at the other table.

One of the officials walked by as I was shuffling the cards. "What happened?" I asked him.

He informed me, "Mr. Sleater needed a few points to go out and made a quick knock, but Mr. Shubin undercut him."

Acting strictly on a hunch, I made a mental note that I would not risk losing the game by an undercut. I would wait for Lassman to knock or I'd get gin on him.

It was a decision I was never to regret.

After a few minutes I was able to knock. But I didn't. A few plays later Lassman picked a card from the deck and dropped it face down—meaning it was a hot card. Instead of putting it in his hand and studying it and taking his time, he seemed to panic and threw it in the discard pile.

I picked it up faster than I ever picked up a card in my life, went gin—and I was in the finals.

Later I met Lassman. He was wandering around in a daze mumbling, "I should have won . . . I should have won."

He sorrowfully related that he had his cards analyzed and that if I hadn't played my intuitive flash and had knocked, he had a layoff on my hand that, while it wouldn't have given him the game, would have stopped me from going out.

Etta and Karen had watched every move. While my daughter didn't fully comprehend the game, all she had to do was watch her mother's face to know whether I was ahead or behind.

I took an hour's break before the finals. This would be a 500 pointer that would decide the International Gin Rummy Championship.

"Any criticism?" I asked Etta, downing my second glass of milk.

"Just one. Midway in the game you drummed on the table."

It was then that I heard Karen comment to another child her age, "An' my daddy is the best gin rummy player in the whole, big, wide world."

I kissed her, whispering into her ear, "Not yet, Honey," and five minutes later I sat down to play the most important match of my life.

I was barely conscious of the overflow audience, although periodically—generally during shuffling—I could hear some protracted oohs and aahs, and once a woman's shrill scream (not my wife's) penetrated my thoughts.

For the most part, though, I shut out every thought except the game itself. My mind wasn't dwelling on my shrinking bankroll, which was down to sixty-seven dollars and some odd cents. In fact, so total was my concentration that it had not yet registered that I was already guaranteed at least second place with its prize of five thousand dollars. Even Etta was not conscious of it. Afterwards we realized I could have borrowed against the minimum of the five thousand I had coming to bet on myself, as many players did. But that was afterwards. During the game itself, it was as though the Chet Wander sitting at the table was a totally different person I had created solely for the purpose of scoring 500 points first.

The first half of my game with Shubin seesawed back and forth. I jumped into an early lead; then Shubin passed me up and held the lead with 310 points. They were the last points he scored in the game. I forged out in front closer and closer to the magic 500 mark.

As my lead against Shubin widened, I employed some of the tactics a good gin player loves to use but can only afford to when he feels solid ground under his feet. I was able to speculate on a few cards, something I ordinarily would not do three times in a whole week of play. Once I picked up a card as a decoy to throw my opponent off balance, discarding it a few plays later. I was able to "fish" for cards, throwing out a key card as bait for another card I wanted.

All I needed was one big hand to cinch my win. On the last hand, my cards shaped up early in the game, and I needed just one card to fill it in. I geared my play to getting a card that would complete my third meld. On the fifth play of the hand, Shubin discarded a 7. I went gin with three 7s, the 4-5-6 of spades, and the 9-10-Jack-Queen of spades.

I was the Champion of the World.

When victorious in a gin battle, you don't jump the table like you do over a tennis net. You rise and grasp the hand of your opponent and mutter "tough luck." The indoor athletes never head for the showers as their outdoor brethren do. The winner takes a little water, but it's as a chaser or mixed into a victory drink.

The loser has already taken a bath.

Hail to the Champ!

2

Flashbulbs went off and cameras snapped me gazing fondly at ten thousand silver dollars piled high on a table, while I clasped the trophy of World Championship. Upon my head was a crown displaying the final winning hand.

Shubin was awarded five thousand dollars for finishing second.

My favorite photograph of the many that were taken shows Karen standing on the tabletop laden with ten thousand silver dollars, giving me a proud kiss on the cheek. After the ceremonies were over and the cash was being wheeled away, Karen let out a wail, "Don't let them take my Daddy's money away!" It was hard to explain to her that the little piece of paper they handed me in its place was really the same thing.

But if her five-year-old mind couldn't quite grasp it, mine could. Any physical letdown I had suffered from tournament strain vanished the moment I held that beautiful piece of paper in my hand.

I had done no wagering on the side, but many others had bet on me and they were handsomely rewarded. A couple stopped me, offering congratulations and thanks.

"For what?" I asked.

"For a lovely vacation," the woman said. Her husband explained, "We bet on you."

I was curious to know why they took a chance on me instead of Lassman or Shubin.

The lady's answer was: "You seemed in complete control of your nerves and your concentration was marvelous."

Someone speaking of me once remarked, "The room could catch on fire when he's playing and he wouldn't be conscious of the blaze until the water from the fireman's hose swept the cards from the table."

The *Las Vegas Sun*, whose editor, Hank Greenspun, toppled in the final rounds, ran a banner headline comparable to a declaration of war:

WANDER WINS GIN TOURNEY

A balding home decorator from Fullerton, California, beat out a Canadian real estate broker in the finals of the International Gin Rummy Tournament at the Desert Inn last night for a whopping top purse of $10,000.

I was first in line at the bank the next morning, a half hour before the doors opened. I wired money orders to my creditors and had enough left over to reinvest in my business.

Gamblers approached me and offered me a thousand dollars expense money to travel to Louisville for a tournament to play certain unnamed persons in a series of matches. For this I was to receive a percentage. I politely declined. Not being in the card business for a living, I couldn't just pick up and say, "Okay, I'll go with you for a couple of weeks." A few thousand isn't going to offset what may happen to your business if you neglect it. If somebody were to make the offer, "I'll give you $50,000 over a certain period of time for playing a series of matches or exhibitions," why, that would be a different story.

If anyone backed me for a large sum of money I don't think he'd be taking too much of a risk; against ninety-five per cent of the players I believe I'd have an edge. With the other five per cent it might be touch and go. I know what should be done percentage-wise—and I do it. I feel that no player in the world over a period of time could actually beat me.

Before I left town a shady appearing character, who looked like the FBI should be breathing down his neck, tried to steer me into a big stakes game. "You're the champ," he kept repeating, "you won't have any trouble beating these pushovers."

This is the sort of trap to sidestep. I've always been a loner at gin—the safest way to be—and I wouldn't chance playing against people unknown to me. To use a timeworn warning: "Don't play with strangers!"

Winning at Gin

I had left Fullerton just an average guy down on his luck. I came back a celebrity. Telegrams and letters flooded us. My fame must have spread to the post office, because my postman told me that he was a poor card shuffler and asked if I would teach him how. I got out of that one by telling him, "It's just the same as sorting letters, only faster. Keep practicing."

The telephone rang constantly. "H'ya, Champ!" was the customary salutation.

A hand-printed sign tacked to our front door by a neighbor boy who mowed our lawn greeted:

> WELCOME BACK, OH CHOSEN ONE,
> FINEST IN THE ART OF GIN RUMMY.
> CONGRATULATIONS AND GREETINGS,
> WORLD'S CHAMPION!

William E. Boeing, Jr., the airplane manufacturing magnate, had won sixteen thousand dollars by bidding on a group of players of which I was one in a pre-tourney auction. We call this a cardcutta. He turned his winnings over to charity. Mr. Boeing wrote me the following:

> Dear Mr. Wander:
>
> Enclosed you will find my check in the amount of $312. This check is solely a gift and not to be considered part of your taxable income. I certainly want to congratulate you again on your splendid win in Las Vegas.
>
> I imagine you had a lot of fun since returning home after the Tournament. I am a little curious as to whether or not it is easy for you to get a game with your friends without spotting them some sort of handicap, because of your champion status.
>
> I had a lot of fun telling people about the Tournament up here in Seattle, and can only guess that next year it should double in size.
>
> Best wishes to you and your family.
>
> Sincerely,
> William E. Boeing, Jr.

Mr. Boeing's comments about spotting handicaps to my friends was ironic. It was a good while before I could even *get* a game with my friends. I was in great demand as a partner, but a wallflower as an opponent.

Another letter came from a man in New York City who had owed me money for over ten years.

Hail to the Champ!   27

Dear Chet:

> Enclosed find my check for $50.00. It's been so long that I decided to ignore this obligation, but upon learning that you are now the Champion Gin Rummy player of the world, I'm proud and happy to pay off the debt so I can have your endorsement on the back of the check and be able to show it to my friends.

Suddenly I became not only a minor celebrity but a celebrity to the celebrities. Mitch Hamilburg, the noted theatrical agent, said, "Chet, I want to get you together with Mike Frankovich (the motion picture producer) at Charley Farrell's Racquet Club."

Soon I was playing with Zeppo Marx of the Marx Brothers, Desi Arnaz, Jack Kelly of "Maverick," Joan Davis, Mike Souchak the golf champion, and a host of other nimble gin devotees.

In addition, I was sought after by many prominent industrialists, manufacturers, and oil men. I was curious about why these people, so highly successful in their own fields, were so interested in pitting their skills against mine over the gin rummy table. I found that the reasons fell into basically three categories:

(1) To be able to say, "I played against the champion."
(2) To have me for a partner.
(3) To beat the champion.

The third group reminded me of the old Western days when everyone wanted to knock off Billy the Kid, Ringo, and other notorious quick-draw gunmen.

Friends and acquaintances developed a feeling of pride that they knew somebody who had become a *somebody*. One man told me that he had chatted with President Eisenhower when he held the highest office in the nation, and during lulls in conversations he used to drop this important name.

"I've eliminated Ike now," he informed me, "and I use your name instead."

There were scores of persons I had played with sporadically who puffed out their chests and proclaimed, "It's amazing, and I used to beat him all the time."

After repeating this statement often enough they actually began to believe it.

Still fresh in my mind is the first game I played after coming home from Las Vegas. A builder friend invited me to his club in Pasadena for dinner. There was a wait before dinner, so he suggested some gin. He introduced me to two other players, one the owner of a coast-to-coast van line.

"We'll play a little game for a quarter," my host proposed.

A quarter of a cent per point was smaller than I usually play for, but of course I was agreeable. Forty-five minutes later dinner was announced, so we settled up. One of the men handed me $265.00. I looked at him incredulously before it suddenly dawned on me that we had been playing for twenty-five cents a point.

This was a larger amount than I had ever played for. I said before, and I'll repeat again, I don't actually play to gamble. I enjoy playing socially where I can have a good time without having huge sums of money involved. There's a vast difference between playing solely to make money and playing for fun. More than gambling for gambling's sake, a good gin rummy game becomes, to me, a challenge to my mentality. I love to pit my mind against other minds. What I'm primarily trying to prove is that I can hold my own, or better, against anyone else. And this can apply to many things besides gin. A healthy spirit of competition is, to me, the essence of the game.

Should I lose to a player, I want to play him again right away —and beat him. Naturally, when I win I receive the usual satisfaction of victory.

It is claimed there are born losers in this world. No matter what they do they can't win. Illustrating this is a story: A gin player knocked with eight points and asked his opponent, "What do you have?" His opponent replied, "I have seven." So of course our "born loser" lost. A few hands later he knocked again with two, asking, "What do you have?" His opponent said, "One." So he lost again. In the very next game he picked up a gin hand, proudly laid it out on the table, and said, "I have gin. *Now* what do you have?" The other player said, "I have twelve cards."

You also hear of born winners, but no jokes are designed about them. Actually there are no born winners or born losers in gin. The losers are the wild, reckless, devil-may-care players; the winners are the calm, cautious, percentage players.

I'm going to teach you how to become a winner.

Where before it had taken six months of constant drilling to convince these gin addicts they had to play systematically, it now took about one minute. I'd overhear remarks from other tables such as, "Chet wouldn't have played it that way."

I moved from the doghouse to the Taj Mahal.

Not only wasn't it necessary to pound common sense into them any more; they now openly solicited advice from me, and I fed it to them in copious quantities so that they could integrate it into their play and it would act as an equalizer. I eventually proved that the pattern was the only successful way. Over-all play of the players steadily improved to the point where many times the only difference between any of us was a good run of cards instead of a bonehead play.

One of the worst offenders in our group was an astute business man and careful investor, who would think twice before sinking his money into even a gilt-edged proposition. But his gin playing made the most venturesome daredevil look like a Casper Milquetoast. He'd hold two Kings and two Queens—just as if they were of royal families who couldn't be separated—right down to the end.

I poured advice into his deaf ears. After my success at Las Vegas he listened. The following year he went to the International Tournament, where he needed only one game to reach the group of finalists. His opponent for that game was a woman, and when it was almost time to begin the game he found her in the hotel bar having a drink. At the moment she seemed more interested in bar gin than tournament gin, because she told him, "Go ahead, claim a default on the game." But my friend chivalrously insisted that she play the game. She was finally persuaded. She won, and although her over-all record was not good enough to mean anything, the game knocked my friend out of the final rounds.

If you have card sense and perception, you can tell—without being a seer—the pattern of the other player's hand after a few picks, watching his discards and the placement of cards he's pulled from the deck. True, you may miscalculate a card here or there, but you'll have his hand pretty well pegged.

I can't exactly define what a politician means when he calls himself "a conservative." In gin, however, you should be a conservative and that I can define: It means, purely and simply, play percentages.

Why a man is conservative in business and in a flash turns

reckless in cards is beyond my power of comprehension. In business he avoids unsound risks like the plague. Ask him why and he'll tell you, "If I didn't I'd get slaughtered."

Yet this same man gets slaughtered regularly every Friday night in a gin rummy game dictated by his own reckless tactics, sometimes made doubly painful by a run of bad luck.

When I lose I usually lose six, eight, ten, possibly fourteen points. If I knock in the first half-dozen picks against a wild player, I'll reap between twenty-five and forty-five points. I figure if I can win eight hands from an opponent I'm going to win two hundred points, and he has to win more than a dozen to conquer me.

The reckless players go for gin, and that's the old story over and over again. They play their own hand—without considering the other fellow's hand—and usually play for gin.

If you play with only gin fixed in your mind, you have to have tremendous luck to win. I've seen this happen many a time: A player will be ready to knock on the fifth pick while I've got fifteen to twenty unmatched points in my hand. What does he do? Flying in the face of logic, he talks himself into trying for gin. Two or three picks later, my hand is very likely to be as good as or better than his. I may knock and pick up the win. I may be in a position to undercut if he knocks. Or I may have gained enough additional information about his hand to be able to block it against any possibility of reaching gin, which gives me an opportunity to try for gin myself. One thing you can be sure of: I won't make the same mistake he did and stubbornly hold out for gin as an automatic course regardless of the circumstances. Don't forget, it is important to gain information about what your opponent is holding in his hand and play around this information, and not just automatically throw out cards because they are of no immediate use in your hand.

Occasionally, if I've taken a comfortable lead or felt out my opponent until I know his style of play, there are certain hands I'd play for gin against him even though a knock opportunity might occur first. But I must feel that I have an edge and a knowledge of which cards are out. I would have a pretty good idea what cards my opponent needs to fill his hand, and I may be holding a couple of them in runs. Also, my extra card may be a layoff in case my opponent should knock before I reach gin.

Countless times I've seen the man on the opposite side of the table from me play for gin when he had no chance of going gin. And if he finally decided to knock, by that time I'd undercut him.

When I first began playing in two hundred point games, I sometimes would hear a tiny voice of temptation whisper, "Don't be chicken. Gamble. Go for gin." I'd heed the advice and lose the game. I soon learned to control that impulse.

This may come as a shock to many players, but I would be satisfied to gin twice in playing a dozen games. I consider that good. Based on run-of-the-mill circumstances where nobody is streaking, this is a fair proportion.

Should you be streaking (getting good hands and the other fellow poor ones), two things happen: You can throw almost anything and he won't take it; on the other hand, practically anything he throws you take. This is the equivalent of betting on three horses in a row and having them all win handily.

Many players—despite the fact they have been playing at the game for years and supposedly should know better—play a straight offensive game, with little or no thinking involved. Cards that are of no immediate use to their hand are discarded as rapidly as possible; their only concern is to fill in their own hand, no matter what.

These people are not playing gin—only going through the motions. Against a good player they are not even gambling—they don't have a chance. Against players of their own ilk, it is a matter of who gets the cards he requires first by the luck of the draw or thoughtless discards of opponents.

On the other hand, a player can play too defensive a game. He too will eventually lose to the sound player, although his "frightened" play will hold down his losses. He needs more heart, courage—or call it what you will—but he should not play to win money either, only for relaxation and entertainment.

When I first started playing gin with my wife, she was an average player who played strictly on instinct, feminine intuition, hunches —only for the cards she wanted, totally unconcerned about what I might be holding in my hand. Now I will back her against any player anywhere at any time. She listened. She learned. She now knows what to do and when to do it and has the knack of being able to diversify her game.

The Name of the Game 35

In the beginning, just like everybody else, she was skeptical when I taught her how to play and coached her in the fine points. I'm sure she thought she married a lunatic. But after weeks of regimentation, patience, and discipline, she elevated her game to the expert class.

Gin rummy playing between husbands and wives is of course very widespread. Usually no money changes hands, but the appeal comes, I suppose, from the natural competitive spirit between the sexes. It's a healthy way of expressing the struggle for superiority that has existed between men and women for as long as men and women have existed. I wouldn't advise many married couples, if they want to sail through the sea of matrimony without capsizing the boat, to compete against each other in high stakes games. That can be carrying the competitive spirit too far.

A perennial story around the gin tables concerns a domestic triangle. The husband comes home unexpectedly from a business trip to find his wife and best friend together.

"How can you do this to me?" he asks his friend angrily.

"Can't we settle this like gentlemen?" the friend pleads.

The husband mulls it over, deciding, "We can. Let's play a game of gin for her."

"Okay," agrees his friend, "but let's bet five cents a point on the side to make it interesting."

To be conservative playing gin doesn't mean you'll play a colorless, wishy-washy game. Only a sensible one. You can still attack with the ferocity of a panther. Actually, you're upgrading your game. You'll command more respect for your ability, which shows proof in the final score tally.

Would you, in your middle age, take off down a steep hill with a skateboard strapped to each foot? Of course not. Trying to gin each hand amounts to the same thing. The only difference is that your pocketbook gets bruised instead of your body.

Remember: Gin is only the name of the game.

Education of a Card Player

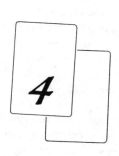

I believe I was inadvertently exposed to gambling by my mother. The Mah-Jongg craze struck Albany, New York. As a youngster of fourteen I was fascinated, upon coming home from school, to hover over the table loaded with tiles and racks in our family parlor and hear such alien terms as two bam, four crack, and west wind roll off the tongues of the assembled women.

Studying a Mah-Jongg card, I soon learned the rudiments of the game, progressing to a point where, when my mother adjourned to the kitchen to serve milk, tea, cakes, and fruit, I substituted for her. Within the space of the first minute an invisible needle seemed to prick my skin, sending a raging gambling fever into my body.

One day I won twenty-two thousand dollars cutting high card with a classmate. Of course we never settled up. This triumph prompted me to remark, "Gambling is great fun."

"You were just lucky," my friend grumbled—a comment that would be forthcoming hundreds of times in the future.

"Sure," I admitted. "Gambling is nothing but luck."

How wrong I was!

Other forms of gambling led me to playing tennis with the town drunk for a nickel per game, after first waiting for him to sober up. I played chess, checkers, and then rummy.

Playing for mere fun didn't quench my gambling thirst. It was, I discovered, far more exciting when something was at stake. I remember once I played poker, while going to high school, staying in every pot to the last call.

We played in an unheated garage. The weather outside was freezing. I had borrowed my older brother's bearskin coat, a popular type of garment for keeping warm in northern New York in this period. I lost it by calling a full house with three of a kind.

Over a period of time my brother unwittingly supported me. I lost a saxophone of his—something the neighbors didn't mind a bit. Next came a tennis racket, followed by a catcher's glove. My poker was atrocious, a game I had learned from kibitzing behind my father's chair. To my mind my father was the greatest man who ever lived, but little did I realize that he was no card player.

"My father's just a tough luck player," I thought.

No one had ever explained the facts of gambling life to me.

The urge to gamble increased—to gamble on everything, regardless of the odds against me.

Actually you couldn't call what I was doing gambling, because I had only an infinitesimal chance of ever winning. Unless a person has full knowledge of odds and percentages, he isn't gambling; he's only throwing money down the well. It's just a matter of how much he has in his pocket and how long it's going to take to rid himself of it and get it into the other fellow's pocket.

In such cases, where you haven't been introduced to percentages, it is better to hand over the money to charity so that at least it goes to a person less fortunate than you.

If you don't play percentages and are perfectly honest, sensible, and adult in your thinking, rationalize the loss that is sure to come by accepting the fact: "I'm going to toss away twenty bucks tonight rather than take my wife out for drinks and dinner."

Then you know what you're doing.

YOU'RE BUYING ENTERTAINMENT.

But conversely, if you sit down and presume gambling is a matter of luck and try to win by playing every hand in poker or forever trying for gin, you're intending to lose money. And you will, because you'd be the kind of person the gambler would be waiting for.

Should you need the action to fill some empty void, it's a narcotic, and the best course for you to take is seek a couch in a psychiatrist's office. His fee will be stiff, but if he effects a cure you'll save money in the long run.

An example of the narcotic-gambler type was displayed by a friend of mine who accompanied me to the horse races at Santa Anita. He won almost a thousand dollars betting on the first race. I counseled, "Bob, why don't you wager a nominal sum on the next eight races and even if your luck is bad you'll go home with a profit of seven or eight hundred dollars."

I considered this a fine addition to his income for a day of pleasure.

He stared at me like I was an escapee from a mental institution. "Listen," he said sharply, "it isn't *my* money, it's *their* money. Why should I tighten up?"

"It's *your* money," I tried to point out. "It's in *your* pocket. It belongs to *you*."

Shaking his head and muttering to himself, he started toward the hundred dollar window. The upshot of it was that at day's end he lost the thousand of what he claimed was "their money" plus four hundred of his own.

If you know the percentages and gamble, it's bona fide gambling. Should you, the reader, and I flip a coin five hundred times, both of us know the percentages and they're fairly even. That's what I call real gambling. Then luck, and only luck, determines the winner.

Lots of things originate in Brooklyn; why not a gin rummy player? It was here, as a fledgling—a young man who had had a bad run of gambling luck (I thought)—that I received an education in the fine art of gambling and, in particular, gin rummy.

Parkville, in Brooklyn, was a social club, a combination of ping pong, tennis, cards. I was eighteen years old, working for an uncle in Brooklyn who was in the chemical business. Card play at Parkville was not considered part of the recreational program. In a room upstairs it was an extracurricular activity. Only gin was played.

I'd lose oftener than I'd win. I noticed that certain fellows seemed to win more than others, and one older man won regularly. I wondered why. Quitting the game, which had become a nightly fixture in my life, I started standing behind his chair. I could hardly believe my eyes. How, I wondered, could anyone play so lousy, yet win so consistently. It had to be luck.

Education of a Card Player

I studied his every play assiduously. But there was no break-through in my thinking, no dawning on my mental horizon that he was playing any way but foolishly. My idol suddenly had feet of clay. He was an incredibly bad player enjoying a phenomenal streak of luck.

One day everything became crystal clear. It was as if I had been viewing a blurred image in a cloudy mirror and suddenly the glass cleared. This man, I realized, was playing disciplined gin and strictly percentages, while varying his game periodically. I moved a little closer until I was practically breathing down his neck. He didn't seem to mind.

I began to understand how he played. He'd have two deuces (spade and diamond) and the 4 of diamonds. The 2 of hearts had already been discarded. He had, therefore, two chances to draw a card that would complete a meld: 2 of clubs or 3 of diamonds. The 3 of spades was also in the discards, so he knew that the 2 of spades was a safe throw. He threw it instead of throwing a wild five which left him with a 2 and 4 of diamonds. Now, rather than having two chances to complete his meld, he had only one. But—he had thrown a card he knew his opponent could not use.

His opponent drew a 3 of diamonds from the deck. Analyzing it, he concluded, "Well, the 3 of spades is out, so the 3 of diamonds is fairly well protected." He threw it into the discard pile.

My teacher picked it up and went gin.

Naturally, his opponent commented, "Boy! are you lucky. One chance and you get it."

But it wasn't just the one chance he claimed it to be. Far from it. My teacher created the situation by controlling the direction of the game and shaping his own destiny. He'd seen that certain cards would become available from the deck, and he had figured the percentage chance of picking up what he needed while at the same time holding his opponent at a standstill by throwing only safe cards.

In the meantime, while his opponent was throwing the "safe" 3 of diamonds, he may have been sitting with two 4s and a 6. If my teacher had thrown that wild 5 it might have enabled his opponent to go gin. So my teacher was actually accomplishing three things simultaneously: He was preventing the other player from filling his hand, possibly keeping him from winning the hand, and prolonging the game while he gave himself a chance to improve his own hand to the winning point.

Another lesson I learned was this: I might have three completed melds in my hand (4-5-6 of spades, 3-4-5 of diamonds, 3 Aces) and an odd deuce. We're three-quarters of the way down the deck. My opponent knows what I've got and I know what he's got. I know that my odd deuce is a layoff on one of his melds, and that his odd card is a layoff on one of mine. If I knock I'm going to get undercut, and if he knocks he's going to get a dose of the same medicine.

So what I'd have to do—depending on what the knock card was —is to break up one of my melds. In this case, I'd throw one of the Aces—preferably the Ace of diamonds, since I have the 3 of diamonds to protect it.

Let's say I pull in a 3 of clubs on my first draw. In the next two picks I would discard my other two Aces. Meanwhile, the chances are splendid that I would pick up another card to go with the 3 of clubs, plus another odd card. I can still make gin in a different way, or at least end up with a solid hand. Mainly, though, I'm protecting my hand against an undercut that would lose me twenty-five to thirty points.

I also gained the valuable knowledge that the man whose play I was studying would rather make a hand go all the way down the deck than take the chance of throwing a wild card and losing the game.

My thinking became revolutionized. Until my nightly lessons started behind his chair, I was certain I knew the game. Now the errors in my previous thinking stood out boldly. From my kibitzer position I hardly dared clear my throat or blow my nose for fear I'd be banished. To be removed was comparable to expulsion from college. That walk to stand behind his chair was to me the same as crossing the Atlantic Ocean to study at Oxford University on a fellowship.

After one month I felt I had gained my diploma, graduating cum laude.

At the conclusion of an evening session, my mentor rose from his chair, faced me and asked, with a twinkle in his eye, "Young fellow, are you learning anything?"

"Plenty, sir," I said.

"Can you put into practice what you've learned and stick to it?" he questioned.

"I'm going to try."

He smiled. "If you can, I'll finally get some competition around here."

For me it was the time for decision. I felt qualified to compete against any opposition, although I still had much to learn from experience. But I had to make a choice. I could play for fun, figuring it would cost me some money, or I could play correctly for profit, sticking to percentages.

I made my decision, and within a short time I rose from the amateur to the expert class.

After my tutelage at Parkville ended and I went forth with my G.R. degree in hand, I started to play again, ever mindful of my lessons. On evenings when I didn't have to work the next day I did some marathon playing, sitting down at 7:00 P.M. and continuing straight through until ten the next morning. In those games there was a flexible time limit. "We'll quit at eleven," everybody chorused; and then when that hour struck on the clock and someone was stuck, time was discarded—although usually the player begging for a time extension to get even proceeded to lose three or four times as much.

Many persons standing over the green felt tables in Las Vegas also have a limit, but it's money lost and not time. An average tourist has a figure fixed in his mind: "If I lose two hundred, I'll quit." A gambler can't. If he wins, he wants more; if he loses, he wants to recoup. As my mother used to say, "They want to take home the tablecloth."

A conservative Las Vegas player bets, for example, ten dollars. He wins. He lets it ride and he has forty. Then, good judgment prevailing, he might withdraw thirty, betting only ten. This type of player rarely gets hurt and, if luck smiles favorably upon him and he doesn't tarry too long at the table, he may make part of his weekend expenses.

But to be on the safe side, always have a tankful of gas in your car.

The seasoned gambler—usually recognizable by his eyes, unsmiling face, steady hands—can, with a lucky streak, bruise a casino owner. He doubles and triples his bets, backing them up behind the line until his hot hand is halted by the official brake:

reaching the house limit. Even though the house may wince a bit, the over-all effect is charged off to good advertising since this is not a usual occurrence. Tourists go home and relate the exploits of this gambler and often say, "Why, he won five thousand dollars and I was standing right next to him!"

This helps stimulate an avalanche of new tourists with fresh money, trying to emulate the feat.

It takes considerable nerve to defy the odds and percentages and let your money ride. Before my Parkville lessons I had a few flings at it. Not today. The odds escalate too astronomically. But the gambler—whose credo is "easy come, easy go"—instead of heading for the highway with his winnings will probably reappear early next morning and give most of it back again to the house.

There are players at Las Vegas who, quick as a flash, are in over their heads. "Just one more roll is all I need," they think. But it's another roll, and still another, and so on. In Glendale, California there's a personable young man named Jack Hanlon in the car business who found himself in the situation just mentioned but luckily escaped to see his bankroll live another day.

He was playing roulette alongside a girl who had bought ten dollars' worth of chips, which she promptly lost playing the red or the black. Noticing that she was disconsolate and also beautiful, the Glendale man soothed her by saying, "Don't worry, honey, I'll get back your money for you."

He placed $10.00 on the red and lost, $20.00 on red and lost, $40.00 on red and lost, $80.00 on red and lost, $160.00 on red and lost again. Now he had to bet $320.00 to redeem the stranger's $10.00. It was his last chance, because the house limit of $500.00 would stop him before he could double up again. Luckily he won his final bet. Otherwise he would have been out $630.00 simply to recoup $10.00 which wasn't even his.

His friend and traveling companion, Larry Gilhooley, a witness to the struggle, left to catch a show. When he returned to his room at about 2:00 A.M., he found Hanlon climbing into bed.

"How did you make out with the girl?" he questioned.

"Girl? What girl?"

"Why, the girl you tried to win ten dollars for," he said.

"Oh," the car salesman said, shuddering slightly. "Well, to tell you the truth, I was too nervous after risking all that money to even think of her after it was all over."

I relate this story to illustrate how the pursuit of a small amount of money can often lead to trouble. Relative to gin, the moral is: If you're in a bad losing streak, don't try to increase the stakes. You may not be as lucky as the man from Glendale was.

How much luck has to do with gin is a question I've been asked countless times. I don't believe it's possible to furnish exact estimates. There is no yardstick, no measuring rod, nothing on which to base accurate figuring.

Too many players enjoying a run of extraordinary luck pop a button off the vest and attribute it to superior playing. The ego begins to swell to a point where it distorts clear, logical thinking. They don't recognize the fact that Lady Luck is a fickle dame who comes calling on unscheduled visits, sometimes hanging around for quite a spell and at other times making a sudden exit.

One time I had a progressive run of bad luck playing against my wife. I couldn't beat her. I changed my style, but to no avail. Without warning—which is always the case—luck started to come my way and I could do no wrong. If I'd looked under my chair I might have found a thirty-two carat diamond. If I'd laid my cards down—needing only one to go gin—and a tornado burst through the open window, the cards would have remained undisturbed. If I'd crossed a freeway blindfolded during the rush hours, not a car would have touched me.

Luck is something intangible. If we knew what brings it on, everybody would have it. But there would still be losers. Someone has to lose. However, that someone doesn't have to be you if you play percentages. You can weather the storm of ill luck by playing percentages and holding your losses to a minimum until Dame Fortune deserts your opponent and moves over to your side of the table.

Louis Nizer, the famed criminal lawyer, author of the smash hit *My Life In Court,* in a previous book titled *Between You And Me* belittles the skill factor in gin rummy. He writes:

"In gin, the factor of skill is so small after it is balanced by basic knowledge of the game by almost all players, that it plays practically no part."

Mr. Nizer even names the chapter "Gin Rummy—the Great American Illusion."

I take exception to Mr. Nizer's contentions.

Let's say that two players compete over a period of time.

Although luck may not even out to exactly, fifty-fifty, with everything involved, the better player will still wind up winning money. If you play the right type of percentage game and just get an average break in the luck angle, you're going to be the winner.

I contend that the superior player always has the edge, whether the game lasts for only an hour or play continues on a slow boat to China. Of course, the longer the game lasts the more apparent the edge will become.

Louis Nizer is a skillful attorney of national repute. If he goes into court against John Jones, freshly graduated from law school, Nizer immediately has the edge, the same as I would have the edge over an average gin rummy player. Now suppose Nizer duels Samuel Leibowitz in the courtroom. The case might be a toss-up and decided by a witness who made one tiny slip in his testimony. Here again is the element of chance and luck favoring the winner.

In refutation of Mr. Nizer's belief that gin rummy is not a game of skill was a decision handed down in the U.S. District Court in Las Vegas on February 23, 1965.

Several days earlier I had received an urgent call from Al Freeman, publicity director of the Sands Hotel in Las Vegas and co-ordinator of the International Gin Rummy Tournament. Al is in no small part responsible for the tournament's success and impressive growth, and he is justifiably proud of his "baby." When Al called me, he had thousands of tournament announcements ready to be sent out—and the roof had literally just caved in on him. The Las Vegas postmaster had advised the Tournament sponsors that they should not use the mails to promote the event because, he claimed, it constituted a lottery. The Tournament officials petitioned for a restraining order to prevent the post office from interfering with the mailing of Tournament announcements, and the case was to be heard on February 19.

I was asked, along with Albert Moorhead and Alfred Shein-wold, to appear as an expert witness supporting the claim that gin rummy is a game of skill and therefore not a lottery. The defense brought in Dr. Ernest Blanche, of a math and statistical firm, formerly a college professor and government statistician. Dr. Blanche told the court that the chance of the same hand being dealt twice was one out of seven million. "Certainly skill and remembrance of cards play a part in determining the winner," he said, "but it is essentially a game of chance or luck."

The position taken by us who testified on behalf of the Tournament sponsors can be summarized in the words of Al Moorhead, who asserted, "I can say flatly that a player using the techniques of memory, 'reading' of the other player's hand, deception, and decoy moves will emerge as the winner. I would not say that a person must have all of these talents to play winning gin. But a person with these abilities will most assuredly beat one without."

The hearing lasted five hours. The next few days, when we were awaiting the outcome, were tense ones for the Tournament officials. With the annual tournament less than a month off, they had already had to delay sending out advertisements and invitations much longer than they would have liked.

The judge announced his decision on February 23. He held that gin rummy was not a lottery as conducted in the Las Vegas Tournament and could therefore be referred to in material going through the mail.

As you can well imagine, many a sigh of relief was heard not only in Las Vegas but throughout the world where aspiring contestants were sharpening up their game for the Tournament.

One thing you may be sure of: Even if the decision had gone against them, the Tournament officials would have found a way to get word around about the Tournament, even if they had to resort to carrier pigeons. Gin rummy fans don't give up that easily.

As your playing improves, your personal skill/luck ratio will tilt more and more in favor of the former.

Everyone is aware that percentage can't be guaranteed to come through consistently. At best, it only provides you with an edge. If I were to take four Jacks and an Ace and shuffle them, the odds are going to be against your picking the Ace on the first or even the second try. Yet it could happen that you will pick the Ace out on your first draw five times in a row. That's real luck. And it's also beating the percentage tables.

A knowledgeable player gains percentage on an average player the moment he observes him pick up his cards and set them in sequences from an Ace on up. He takes them in in a group and sets them. An adroit player can glance at the unmatched cards and instantly know what he has. It takes me about five seconds to set my hand. Unless my opponent is a shrewd player, I can tell his hand pretty thoroughly by the time he has made his first few plays (after first observing if he's right- or left-handed). Let's assume he has an Ace-2-3 and King, Queen, Jack, two 8's, and two 9's. On each pick you can watch where the card he picks goes in his hand and what card comes out and figure the adjacent cards.

A good player gathering his hand together won't place the cards in the same spot every time. He will intermingle his cards. When play starts, every card he picks up from the deck he puts into his hand and resets his hand, moving everything around, even though he may then throw out the card he just picked up.

If you're an average player, you may pick up a card you know you don't need and discard it without ever putting it in your hand. You shouldn't. You've got to take every card, put it into your hand, and move your hand around. Such tactics often scare the hell out of the fellow you're playing with. Any fright displayed by an opponent gives you a psychological advantage.

Such an advantage was once obtained by an acquaintance of mine who didn't exactly have a high code of ethics. He was playing for five cents a point, and the game was running about even. Drawing a card from the deck, he said, "Hold it a moment, will you? I have to go to the bathroom."

He left and stayed ten minutes. Coming back to the table he sat down, picked his hand up, and hollered, "Gin!"

His opponent's eyes bugged and his voice trembled as he demanded, "Why didn't you go gin before?"

This killed off his opponent for the remainder of the day. Seething with suppressed wrath and caught in the grip of terrible frustration, he made many costly errors of play.

Be certain of one thing: Luck is going to run for you and run against you. When against you, it will be necessary to tighten up, playing percentages until the luck pendulum swings back toward you.

You can't, in the long run, beat the percentage players—so join 'em and beat those who don't play percentages.

Gin – Friars Club Style

5

Gin rummy players have been called the largest group therapy crowd in the world. Personally, I don't believe they are curable. Unlike alcoholics, who repeatedly claim—just before they fall sprawling on the floor—"I can take the stuff or let it alone," a gin player never makes such a strong assertion. Once addicted, he knows that he can't kick the habit.

Gin players have penetrated and gained a foothold in every form of governmental, public, and private life. Physically, they are a congenital and unrecognizable group. You can't stand in a crowd, stretch out your arms in any direction and fail to touch one of them. If they were a fifth column infiltrating our nation from a foreign power, the FBI would be powerless unless they knew the one infallible method of detection: riffle a pack of playing cards. This familiar sound, upon reaching their ears, causes a transformation that quickly separates them from other citizens.

Insides seethe with an internal combustion, explodable if not released. Breathing accelerates. Globules of moisture gather on brows. Eyes dart about, subconsciously searching for a table, chair, and a score pad.

Yes, there is something special about a gin rummy player . . . .

There is also something extra-special about the wife or husband of a gin rummy player. Otherwise, long, never ending lines would form in front of divorce courts as gin rummy addicted spouses stayed out later and later at night. Medals should be cast for those wives and husbands who bear the cross. Fortunately, many of them find a happy solution by taking up the game themselves.

Unless you're playing to pick up a tab or the equivalent, gin is essentially a serious game. It's like sitting in a session of the Supreme Court. One of the unwritten rules is to keep your conversation to a bare minimum. This is impossible to enforce. To deprive a player of grousing, grumbling, and complaining is akin to destroying personal liberty should he be losing. On the other hand, how can you keep a winner from telling jokes?

When comedian Phil Silvers sits down to play gin, kibitzers draw close, expecting to hear some choice ad libs. They seldom do. Silvers, one of the glibbest talkers on television, is blanketed by silence. He's all concentration—which he should be—and has no time for bon mots.

Silvers, along with entertainer Tony Martin, George Jessel, Milton Berle, George Raft, the three Ritz Brothers, Joey Bishop, abetted by Los Angeles Mayor Sam Yorty, millionaire chain shoe store owner Harry Karl, President Al Hart of Schenley Distillers Company, plus other names that make the news, play at the Friars Club in Beverly Hills.

Here, in a plush setting governed by club rules, are some of the leading gin rummy luminaries in the United States, a statement that would be instantly disputed by thousands, due to the fact that few players of this game concede to anyone in skill.

Harry Ritz, a round-the-world gin expert, plays what I'd call a "cagey but consistent" game. He plays like an automaton whether he's stuck a hundred points or is four to the good. A losing streak never frustrates him. For variation, he may pick up four cards that won't match any of his sequences, if he has a bad hand. Behind his chair there's often a whisper, "Harry plays a crazy game." He's crazy like the proverbial fox. Undoubtedly, Harry shows a neat profit through the years.

He has his own gin philosophy. He says, "A guy will claim, 'I don't know what it is, but I lose to you every time. I beat everybody else. Not you. You're a jinx!'

"In gin players this complaint is predominant," Harry contends. "There's no such thing as a jinx. The one called 'a jinx' is simply a better player. But who will admit it? Surely not another gin player."

Harry believes that if you lose between fifty and a hundred points you should jump right up and quit. "Just say, 'I'm tired,' or, 'I've sprained my wrist dealing.' Or, 'I've got a cramp.' Back off. Don't give him a chance to beat you for any more. There's always tomorrow and maybe a better run of cards. It's ethical enough," he maintains, "to quit in gin when you feel like it. In poker it's a breach of etiquette."

Much to the delight and profit of the sundry playing card manufacturers, gin rummy is a great game for deck changers. One evening at the Friars Club, while a superstitious player was changing decks for the ninth time within an hour, his opponent asked him, "Wouldn't you like to go back to the first deck?"

The Friars Club has the loser dealing. They feel it's a precaution against possible cheating. Then, they reason, it is impossible for a loser to complain that his opponent is doing any tricky maneuvering of the cards. This same rule prevails in the Las Vegas Gin Rummy Tournament and in many clubs throughout the country, usually for the same reason. It can be a safeguard of sorts, but if a player is really bent on cheating, the methods he can use are so multiple and so varied that there is no absolute protection against it. Even if he is the non-dealer, generally no one will object if he gives the cards an extra shuffle or two before he cuts them. In fact the Las Vegas Tournament extends the non-dealer the right to the final shuffle, and most rules permit it.

Just as the intentional cheater has many opportunities to practice his guile, the honest player who is on the lookout has many ways to protect himself. My own feelings about this are very definite: If I suspect there is any cheating going on, this is a game I don't wish to be in, this is a player I will avoid in the future. I know that if I continue to play him things are likely to get very touchy before the end of the evening. This is decidedly not my idea of a pleasant round of gin rummy, whether money is involved or not.

One of the foremost players at the Friars Club is Ely J. Glassman, a businessman who at one time won the championship of the Beverly Club. A member of the Friars Club rules committee, he explains the attitude of the club toward anyone who is suspect.

"If we find a player is not conducting himself in a legitimate manner, we cut him out immediately. We just refuse to play with him. If he's unable to get into a game he can't cheat. Ostracism is the best policy. None of us here is trying to make a living playing cards."

This has rarely happened at the Friars.

It has often been said that a millionaire will cheat you quicker than a bum in gin. The accepted explanation is that a millionaire, due to his accumulation of wealth and various successes, has a greater ego urge than a bum to be top dog.

The commonest form of cheating in gin is the way your opponent lays his cards down after you knock or go gin. He may say, "Thirty-nine," and slide them face down into the pile, and for all you know he might have had seventy-nine.

Glassman played one of these card sliders at another club. He won handily, although he always had to take his opponent's word for the count.

"Why did you let him continually cheat you?" a perturbed friend, who witnessed the game, asked.

"Oh, well," Glassman said, indifferently, "I was getting a fairly good count and I was beating this fellow pretty regularly. Maybe I wasn't winning as much as I was entitled to, but if I made an issue of it I'd lose an opponent I could handle even if he did cheat."

Aside from the question of avoiding possible cheating situations, there are two schools of thought about who has the slight edge at the start of a hand: the dealer, or the person on the receiving end of the deal. My own feeling is that the receiver has the odds in his favor because he has first choice of picking up the knock card.

The opposite point of view is that the dealer is in a good spot because he receives valuable information before he makes his first play. If the receiver picks up the up card, that furnishes the first clue to what he is holding; the discard that follows is clue No. 2. If the receiver refused the up card, that in itself is informative; and should both players refuse the up card, the receiver still is obliged to break his hand first.

As previously mentioned, a good case can be constructed for either point of view, but I would rather have first crack at the knock card. Many persons regard it as a moot question.

Glassman doesn't mind kibitzers if they are well mannered, resigning himself to the fact that it's more or less acceptable practice to form in a knot behind the chair. They laugh . . . you laugh with them. He feels they're almost part of the game.

He remembers the time he was playing in a game with a kibitzer behind his chair and another behind his opponent's. One kibitzer claimed the count was twenty-three points. The other said twenty-two. The players thought it was twenty-one. An argument started. Everyone became embroiled. There was more action behind the chairs than on the table.

In some instances a player has been known to turn to a kibitzer and say harshly, "Who needs you! Why don't you mind your own business!"

This can cause a kibitzer to sulk—some are barely able to hold back tears—for fear his behind-the-chair privileges will be taken away, causing him to lose a way of life. There is no sight more depressing than a sad kibitzer.

Kibitzers are attracted to gin rummy games like flies to sugar. To me, gin rummy is a contest of skill and judgment between myself and the player on the other side of the table, and I prefer to keep it that way, without benefit of an audience.

If the Friars Club were a bridge club, the players would be segregated into definite classifications: good, poor, excellent. The excellent players wouldn't want to sit down and play opposite poor players as partners. The disproportion can spoil the game.

No such issues arise in gin. In gin everyone imagines he's a champ. In gin no one has a defeatist complex. In gin no player admits another player is superior.

Gin is widely played in resorts and in clubs, but the home players are in the majority. Many times is the remark overheard in hotels, "I'll play you one hand before dinner." A friend of mine from New York who was vacationing in Miami Beach played the customary "one hand before dinner." He not only lost the "one hand," but in the course of trying to get even after dinner, he parted with $5,000.

Some people in a similar situation, in order to ease their troubled minds, might have taken a long stroll across the beach on this moonlit night, or even committed suicide. My friend tried another cure. He went to a late movie in the City of Miami. It was an entertaining comedy, and just as the pains inflicted during the evening were wearing off and he was becoming his old self again, a gin rummy sequence flashed across the screen. Sometimes you just can't win.

The story is told of two lifeguards stationed at a spacious swimming pool playing gin, when a woman bather began yelling for help.

One of the lifeguards cried, "Come on, let's jump in and save her!"

The other protested, "You can't quit! I've got you on a blitz."

Gin flourishes at nearly every athletic, golf, and private club. Each club believes its members, as a team, could defeat any other club. Some of the finest players are found at the Fort Worth Club in Texas, the Commonwealth Club of Richmond, Virginia, and the Beverly Bridge Club, Los Angeles. (Despite the name "bridge," that game is rarely played here.)

Major domo of the Beverly Bridge Club is Jack Caillie, an expert in his own right. Caillie has received long distance telephone calls from all over the United States from players who wish him to act as arbitrator to settle disputes.

"Common sense should decide all rulings," he contends.

Caillie's club has a lengthy lounge, comfortable couches, individual rooms for play. Green foam rubber covers the tables. The atmosphere is quiet, the emphasis on concentration. For Caillie himself concentration is a second sense. He can put his cards down, leave the table for ten minutes to discuss a business affair, return and still remember—aided by his photographic memory—every card in the discards.

He allows no drinking of hard liquor at his club, theorizing that "whisky and cards don't mix."

It requires more than just the price of membership dues to join the Beverly Bridge Club. Members are admitted only after recommendations, and even then they are carefully checked out by Caillie.

One night Caillie was a spectator at a game held at another club. It will live long in his memory. It was for enormous stakes, and player A had never beaten player B. Player B knocked at a decisive moment. Player A looked at his hand and exclaimed, "No good, you're undercut." Player B fell forward, his head striking the table.

A doctor pronounced him dead.

Player A moaned, "That just shows how unlucky I am. I finally win and the guy dies on me."

Caillie, who witnessed a quarter of a million dollars change hands one evening at his club, has a single sentence of advice to pass on to gin rummy players:

"Never underestimate an opponent."

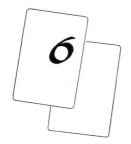

6 Some Do's and Don'ts

An electric juggernaut has come crashing into the world, changing the lives of millions. It is a wheel of fate whose efficiency has had tremendous impact on global conditions. The name is AUTO-MATION. Unemployment lines swell on account of it.

But its effect on the game of gin rummy is trifling.

Since gin surged to the fore in 1939, to snowball and infatuate millions of persons with its brand of excitement, zest, and action, there have been few modifications. True, variations of the game sprouted, as the fast-growing rummy family now numbers hundreds; yet if your grandfather played the game at its inception and did a Rip Van Winkle for twenty years, he could sit down today and not be lost despite the passage of time.

Beaten, he would still claim, "You were lucky."

What your grandfather perhaps didn't discern is that to be tops in the game takes instinct, desire, practice, and study, in addition to having one hundred per cent control of your faculties, sufficient sleep, stomach in good condition, brain nimble.

For practice, it is a good policy to deal two hands and play one against the other. In order to do this you must pick up one hand, close your mind to the other one, and make your play. Then do the same with the other hand. These mental gymnastics oil your brain. Admittedly, this takes a particular kind of mental discipline, and not everyone can do it. But if you can, it's a great way to improve your game.

Another form of practice is shuffling. This may sound ridiculous and cause you to ask, "Who can't shuffle cards?" The answer is that many persons can't do it satisfactorily. When cards are not shuffled thoroughly, a great many return in sequence. And if you just sweated out a poor hand, you certainly don't want to get a portion of it back again.

Cards should be riffled seven or eight times. If you follow numerology, choose your own lucky number of times, as long as it is seven or over. Always have the deck facing downward on the shuffle. If you want to cut a deck two or three times, there is no reason this should offend your opponent. This is your privilege. Don't cut too close to either end of the deck. Deal low, too, so as not to expose the cards. Be certain the bottom card is never revealed.

Changing decks to change luck never helps. A good shuffle may.

Ignore any criticism from an opponent, should he object to your two or three time cutting of the cards. He may caustically remark, "What's the matter, don't you trust me?" If either one of you is suspicious of the honesty of the other, better to seek a game with someone else.

Beware of any player you don't know intimately who casually says, "Here, I've brought a couple of decks of cards." Even though you may witness him breaking the manufacturer's seal, he could have marked them beforehand.

Playing partners in a social game is fine, but should it be for fairly high stakes, it is better to go it alone. A loner does it all by himself, carrying full responsibility on his shoulders, enjoying the plaudits, self-satisfaction, or the money if he wins.

When playing with a group of strangers, many people feel they are safeguarded because they will be rotating partners throughout the evening. This is no guarantee. The other players may be in cahoots as a group, with a pre-arrangement that whichever one is your partner at the moment will just happen to lose.

Partnerships or teams can be a risky alliance for other reasons also. Your partner might be an inferior player. He may enter the game in a highly nervous condition motivated by a business deal that failed or a fight with his wife. Then, in an agitated frame of mind, he may play like there's no tomorrow, which is unfair to his partner, who knows there's going to be a tomorrow and wants to enjoy it without a depletion in his bank account.

Strictly solo winning in anything brings a full measure of gratification.

Slow players can be annoying. They often make opponents fidget and squirm like they are sitting on a hot seat. When a sharp player has an inkling of this weakness, he'll often slacken the tempo to a chess game pace, hoping to aggravate, rattle, and interrupt his opponent's train of thought. At the other end of the scale, excessively fast playing can be just as annoying and rattling to an opponent, because his tendency will be to fall in line and speed up his own play more than is his natural tendency.

Another trick some players may attempt to work on you for the purpose of aggravation is to complain orally that they have nothing. They sigh in tortured agony. They groan. They display Academy Award-winning histrionics. These Thespians are very apt to pick up one card and go gin at any moment.

Simply ignore distress signals.

There are many times when you deliberately throw a card that you know will add to an opponent's run. For example, you may be down a good distance in the deck, and you want to make sure you won't be undercut if you knock. In such a case, let us assume that you know your opponent has three Kings and you feel that he may have two other melds. Should that reasoning be correct, and you throw him a fourth King (which can be a good calculated gamble in certain situations), then obviously he will go gin and you will lose.

However, even if he does go gin it may make only a slight change in your point loss compared to what you would lose if you were undercut. If, on the other hand, your opponent picks up your King and continues to play, then you can be fairly certain that he holds a four-card run, a three-card-run and three odd cards. Now you know that it is a fairly safe bet if you knock with a few points.

Still many fear to do this. They justify themselves by rationalizing, "Well, he's got so and so, and I've got a card he needs. I'll hold it." They aren't always even positive. They may hold a Jack because someone has picked a Jack and they haven't discovered yet if it's to fill in a Jack-Queen-King, ten-Jack-Queen, 9-10 Jack, or three Jacks. And they may wind up holding two or three odd cards.

Suddenly the other person knocks. He can lay off one of his odd cards and he's still stuck with twenty points or so. Or the other party can go gin, in which case no cards can be laid off.

Some Do's and Don'ts

Also, depending on the size of the knocking card, you'll find that by taking a risk of deliberately adding to a run that your opponent may have, you can improve your hand.

You must play a basic pattern, but don't stay with any one play continuously. If you do, your opponent will begin to read your hand as easily as he would a book of enlarged type.

Frequently a player will not only take the fourth card to a run—which would be normal in a hand—but he might take a fifth card. Suppose, with a knocking point of seven, he has three 3s, the 4-5-6-7 of diamonds, and an odd 5, deuce, and Ace. The other player throws the 8 of diamonds. He picks it up, discards his 5, and he now has only the Ace and deuce left in unmatched cards.

This provides him with the opportunity to knock at this juncture, score a few points, and get out of a hand.

Control of your patience is of prime import. Do not allow it to wear thin after an undercutting by an opponent or if you only gained a few points on a previous hand. You may say to yourself, "The hell with a safe game. It's getting me nowhere. The best way to play this fellow is to play for gin." This attitude will cost you many points.

Some players are careless analyzers of their hands. Suppose a player has the 7-8-9 of diamonds and the 9 of spades, and he pulls the 9 of clubs. He may think, "If I pull the 6 of diamonds or the other 9, I have two melds," not realizing that his opponent may also have use for the cards he is waiting for, or they may never show up in the game. But on top of it, he has passed up chances to throw safe cards and to improve his hand in other ways.

Don't ever believe a hand is hopeless. No hand is impossible. Development can come fast. Should you be discouraged by a hand of unrelated cards, remember that in only a few picks this muddle can shape into a winner.

I've previously called your attention to mannerisms. You must control your own and watch for revealing ones in others. A doctor I know won as much money one evening as an office solidly filled with patients for a week would have returned. He noticed that a nerve in the right cheek of his opponent began twitching when he had a bad hand, and the doctor took advantage of the betrayal. The twitch made him rich that night.

Never practice economy by using an old deck of cards. An old deck can be read as clearly as marked cards by an unethical player. A fly speck, a grease stain, a dirty fingerprint on the back of a card—to say nothing of a broken edge—are easily memorized and place you at a disadvantage.

If any opponent who is a stranger to you opens a new package of cards, slowly look through it to ascertain if any cards are missing. Naturally it can be claimed that this was a manufacturer's oversight. If it is intentionally done and you are unaware of it, the cheat perpetrating this underhanded move will, as you can see, have quite an advantage in playing his hands.

Remember the proverbial saying: THE HAND IS QUICKER THAN THE EYE. It works with regularity for a magician, and a clever card cheat is a prestidigitator in his own right. He can, for example, when he puts down his melds, lay down a 10-Jack-King of hearts as a completed meld. Of course this type of thing happens sometimes as an honest mistake. It's only when it happens too often with a particular player that you should be on your guard.

When a boxing referee instructs the fighters to "protect your-selves at all time," he might well be referring to a gin rummy battle. Gin, which is a head-to-head clash, played often in privacy, is a paradise for the unscrupulous. In poker a friend might be able to protect the unsuspecting, but in the privacy of an office or a home when only two go at it, the honest, trusting player might attribute his losses to poor play or bad luck and not to chicanery.

W C. Fields once made a movie titled "You Can't Cheat an Honest Man."

I doubt if he ever played gin.

Pigeons are a strange breed of bird often found nesting around gin rummy tables. No matter how often their wings are clipped they keep returning to the scene of the shearing.

The gin rummy pigeon is highly popular, and there is always a seat waiting him wherever the game is played.

This pigeon—nearly always a loser—ascribes his defeats to rotten luck and is reluctant to giving the players taking his money credit for being superior. He is usually willing to pay a high price for the camaraderie existing around the tables.

If a joke is conceived, he is the target.

I knew such a fellow who played in a group at his country club near San Francisco and was often the dupe in a number of hoaxes.

Before he sat down to play he always made a fixed remark: "When are you boys going to let me win?"

On this particular day, one of his companions said, "I'll bet you one hundred dollars on anything that you want—just name it."

The pigeon's mind raced to come up with something, but before he could speak his friend said, "I'll give you a sure bet. I'll bet that Clarence (one of the waiters) drops dead by midnight."

The pigeon looked aghast. He started to answer but his friend interjected, "Well, that's really too gruesome. I'll offer you a more sensible wager." He thought a moment. "I'll bet you that at twelve noon, give or take a few minutes either way, a jet will zoom down out of the sky over the club."

The pigeon snapped at the offer.

Almost on the stroke of noon, with a shattering roar, a jet buzzed the club, startling the pigeon so that he dropped the hand he was playing. He also dropped the hundred dollar wager—a sure thing for the man who had proposed the bet. There had been an arrangement with a military friend of his—after first synchronizing watches—to buzz the country club at noon.

7

Let's Play the Game

There are two versions of how gin rummy originated. One has the game invented by the Spanish, who named it *Con Quièn*, which was changed by the English to Coon-Can, the slang version being more pronounceable. It spread to Mexico and like marijuana came across the border, where it proved to be a far more popular and legal pastime.

The other claim—and the one generally accepted—is that the game was born at the Knickerbocker Whist Club in New York City, sired by Elwood T. Baker, and was first called "Baker's Gin." The name Gin was suggested by Mr. Baker's son, Graham. The year was 1909.

In 1939, after a slow start, the game spread like a prairie wildfire throughout the nation, becoming an overnight craze and bursting into a popularity that has never diminished. Nervous Hollywood movie moguls found it a relaxing tonic for frayed nerves, and on a clear night voices from private yachts anchored off Catalina could be heard crying, "I knock with three."

Today the gin bug has bitten approximately fifty million American card players of all sizes, shapes, and ages. The bug—highly contagious—infects its victims with an incurable virus, producing a perpetual state of bliss and confidence until every player believes he's an expert.

It is powerful enough to mesmerize strong men, and the formation of a Gin Rummy Anonymous Club would be necessary to effect a cure. Breaking the addiction is as difficult as breaking into Fort Knox.

Proof of the popularity of the game is demonstrated by the script change in the motion picture *Goldfinger*, a James Bond thriller from the pen of Ian Fleming. In the Fleming book the arch villain Goldfinger is cheating at canasta by receiving information on his opponent's hand through a receiving set disguised as a hearing aid, transmitted by his secretary who has a powerful telescope trained on the cards.

Whoever the powers might be behind the adaptation of the book to the cinema, they decided to substitute gin rummy for canasta for reasons of audience appeal.

That gin is a game of intensive concentration is perhaps best illuminated by an anecdote. This concerns a man who, playing for huge stakes, lost for six consecutive sessions. Thoroughly disgusted, he pushed back his chair, stood up and declared:

"Goodnight. I'm going home. This house is unlucky for me and I'll never play here again."

His opponent gently reminded him, "But this *is* your house."

Anyone can play gin rummy. As in learning to drive a car, you can pick up the rudiments very quickly. But that doesn't mean you're ready to take a spin on the freeway. The ordinary player considers that he has graduated from gin rummy school once he knows the difference between knocking and ginning. He then proceeds boldly out into the competitive world of gin rummy, convinced he has the game down pat. Such a player is not playing gin rummy; he is playing *at* gin rummy. Like it or not, he'll be getting lessons as long as he continues to play—but more often than necessary they'll be costly lessons, in the form of trouncings at the table.

As you continue into the remainder of this book, you can make yourself not just a player but a winner. Study my principles of sound play and you can make your entrance—or re-entrance—into the big big world of gin rummy an auspicious and winning one.

If you're a novice at the game, don't be disheartened. Actually, you may have a slight advantage over the old-timers whose bad playing habits are deeply ingrained. You will have less to unlearn before starting off on the sure path to successful play.

To play gin rummy you need two things: A regulation deck of fifty-two cards and an opponent.

Both are simple to obtain.

Gin is basically a game between two players, each of whom is dealt ten cards at the beginning of each hand. The object of the game is to form melds with the cards in your hand. A meld consists of three or more cards of the same denomination, or three or more cards of the same suit in unbroken sequence.

The basic rules of the game are given below.

Gin rummy, like anything involving the participation of millions of people, has developed a number of variations in rules of play and scoring. Just as you will find dozens of versions of certain popular folk songs, you will discover many differences in the game of gin rummy as played by this group or that throughout the world.

The rules of play and scoring given below are the ones I recommend. In my many years of playing gin rummy with thousands of people in all sections of the United States, I have probably sat down to every popular variation. Culled from this experience I have concluded that the following rules are the most satisfactory in ordinary play.

The rules given below are deliberately kept down to the basic essentials. I have not included such fine points as what to do when a card falls on the floor or how to cope with a misdeal. Those are rare occurrences. A formal approach to such irregularities is important, naturally, when you are involved in tournament play. The Las Vegas Tournament of necessity has several pages of rules governing irregularities, and during the tournament itself there are always referees on hand to rule on specific incidents. But in a friendly game irregularities are usually settled on an informal basis by mutual agreement between the players. These rules are meant to give you a simple and concise explanation of the game as I recommend it be played.

The guiding principle behind my rules is to make the game to the greatest degree possible a game of skill. For this reason I recommend a longer game (200 points) than is specified by most other sets of rules. In this connection it is interesting to note that the Las Vegas International Gin Rummy Tournament is presently based on 200 point games (except in the finals, in which the games are even longer, ending with a 500 point game in the final match).

Originally the tournament rules called for 125 point games, but the officials received so many letters from players recommending a longer game that they finally increased it.

I have slanted my rules toward skill in other respects as well. I do not recommend doubling the score when the knock card is a spade. I recommend that the maker of an illegal knock play the rest of the game with his hand exposed, *and* that he be required to knock at the first opportunity. This affords a shrewd opponent with an opportunity for some clever maneuvers forcing the illegal knocker into a knock which he can then undercut.

Following the rules you will find some general comments about them and an explanation of some of the popular variations in the game.

Number of Players

Two.

Deck

Standard deck of 52 playing cards. Ace counts as 1; 2 through 10 have their numerical value. Jack, Queen, King have value of 10 each.

For Deal

Players cut from deck; the player drawing the lower card deals the first hand.

Shuffling

Dealer shuffles, non-dealer cuts. Non-dealer may make additional shuffles, but dealer has option of the last shuffle.

Who Deals

After first hand, loser of hand deals the next hand.

The Deal

Alternately, beginning with the non-dealer, each player is dealt ten cards. The twenty-first card is turned face up in one slot of the gin rummy tray, which is placed between the two players. The remainder of the deck is turned face down in the other slot. The turned up card, unless it is an Ace, is called the knock card, and its value determines the maximum number of points with which the hand can be knocked. If the turned-up card is an Ace, it is called the gin card and the game must be played for gin.

GIN RUMMY TRAY

Play

After the deal has been completed, the non-dealer may pick up the knock card and add it to his hand. If he refuses the knock card, the dealer may pick up the knock card and add it to his hand. If both players refuse the knock card, the non-dealer draws the top card from the turned-down deck and adds it to his hand. Whichever player has made the opening play then discards a card from his hand face up in the discard slot of the card tray (the slot in which the knock card was placed).

Thereafter each player in turn completes a play by adding either the top card from the turned-down deck (sometimes called the stock) or the top card from the discard pile to his hand, and discarding a card from his hand. The player may discard the same card he has just drawn from the stock. At the start and completion of each play, the player should have ten cards in his hand. Only the top card in the discard pile should be visible at any time. Once a player has lifted a card from either the stock or the discard pile, he is considered to have made a play and must now discard to complete his play.

Completion of the Game

Play continues until (a) a player knocks; (b) a player reaches gin; or (c) neither player knocks or goes gin, and it would be necessary to draw the next to last (fifty-first) card from the stock in order to continue play; at this point the game ends in a draw, and neither player receives any score.

The Point Count

Matched cards count zero points; unmatched cards from Ace through 10 count the face value of the card; and picture cards count 10 each. Matched cards are cards which form part of a meld. A meld consists of three or more cards of the same rank (such as three 5s or four Jacks) or three or more cards of the same suit in unbroken sequence (as 5-6-7 of diamonds or 9-10-Jack-Queen of spades).

If an Ace is used in a sequence, it can only be used as low card (such as Ace-2-3); if a King is used in a sequence, it can only be used as high card (such as Jack-Queen-King). No card can be used in more than one meld (for instance the 4 of hearts cannot be used in a set of three 4s and a sequence of 4-5-6 of hearts at the same time.)

Knock or Gin

A player who is able to end the game after drawing a card announces his intention to knock or gin and the total point count of his unmatched cards (unless it is gin), lays down his hand arranged into individual melds and unmatched cards, and discards the eleventh card face down on the discard pile.

A player may knock when, after drawing but before discarding, his unmatched cards total the value of the knock card or less, exclusive of the card he intends to discard. If the opponent has any unmatched cards which can be added to the knocker's melds, he may lay off such cards and they are no longer treated as unmatched cards.

However, layoffs may not be made in the case of gin. If the opponent's total count of unmatched cards (after layoffs) is equal to or less than the knocker's total count, the opponent is credited with an undercut.

If a player makes an illegal knock, the game continues except that the cards of the illegal knocker are exposed to the view of his opponent for the remainder of the hand and he must knock as soon as he is able to.

Scoring Toward Game

1. If the player who knocks has a lower unmatched point count than his opponent, he wins the hand, and score for the hand is the difference in their unmatched point counts.

2. If the player who knocks has an unmatched point count equal to or higher than his opponent, the opponent wins the hand and receives the difference (if any) in the point counts, plus a bonus of 25 points for an undercut. He is also credited with one extra box.

3. The player who goes gin (lays down his hand with all ten cards matched) receives an amount equal to his opponent's unmatched point count plus a bonus of 25 points for gin. He is also credited with two extra boxes.

Scoring After Game

1. Winner of game (player who has won 200 or more points during game) receives game bonus of 200 points, plus the difference between his game point score and his opponent's.

2. Each player receives 25 points for each box he has earned (calculated by adding boxes for each hand won plus extra boxes earned).

3. If one player is scoreless, the winner's total score is doubled.

Hollywood Gin

Hollywood gin differs only in that three separate games are scored while the game is played. When a player wins his first hand of a game, his score is applied to Game One; when he wins his second hand, his score for that hand is applied to Game One and Game Two; when he wins his third and all subsequent hands, his score for each such hand is applied to Game One, Game Two, and Game Three. When either player wins one of the games, no further point entries are made for that game.

If a player reaches 200 points in Game One before his opponent has won any points, the opponent's first winning hand score is applied to Game Two; his second and subsequent winning hand scores are applied to Game Two and Game Three. Each of the three games is scored as though it were the only game being played, and the normal bonuses are applied to each completed game.

Gin Rummy for More Than Two Players

THREE PLAYERS (Captain). Players cut the deck; the player cutting high card becomes the "captain" and plays against the other two players, who are partners. The player cutting second highest card deals and plays the first hand against the captain. He continues to play as long as he wins. When he loses a hand, his partner plays the captain until he loses a hand, and so on, until the game is completed. The game is scored as a regular two-handed game, with the partners being treated for scoring purposes as though they were one player. After the first game is completed, the players rotate for the position of captain, the player who cut the second highest card becoming the second captain.

PARTNERS. With four players, players cut the deck; players cutting low become partners, and players cutting high become partners. The first hand is dealt by players from opposite sides, and thereafter the losing partners deal. Each player plays first one opponent then the other, alternating with each hand. Partners may consult only when a hand has been completed and one partner asks the other to wait for the score before continuing play, or notifies him of the results of a completed hand. No score is entered until both hands of a partnership deal have been completed. The winning side is credited with the net result of both hands. Whenever a hand ends in a draw, it is handled as though it were a score of zero, and is not replayed. Only the winning side in any hand is credited with extra boxes it has earned. Recommended game score for a four-man partnership game is 250 points.

MORE THAN FOUR PLAYERS. Played the same as four-handed partnership except that each player of a side plays the same opponent for a complete game rather than alternating from hand to hand. All members of the side that cuts low deal the first hand. Game score is increased by 50 for each additional two players in the game (300 point game for six players, 350 point game for eight players, etc.). If an odd number of players is involved, odd man (low cut) sits out the entire first game. Thereafter the remaining players rotate in sitting out a game.

The variations in Gin described above are some of the most popular. There are many others. Some that enjoy a share of popularity are: Round-the-Corner Gin, Pinochle Rummy, Elimination Rummy, Five Hundred Rummy, Three-Handed Gin, Poker Gin, and Continental Rummy.

Duplicate Gin

The principle of duplicate gin is that each pair of players plays from a deck set in exactly the same arrangement as the deck for every other pair of players. If there are sixteen players, playing A vs. B, C vs. D, E vs. F, etc., then eight decks of cards will be preset in identical order. Players A, C, E, G, I, K, M, and O all will have the same hand, and Players B, D, F, H, J, L, N, and P will all have the same hand. The knock card will be the same for all eight pairs of players, and cards in the stock will also be in identical order.

Of course, by the time the eight sets of players are two or three plays into the hand, each game will have taken its own direction, depending on the skill and judgment of the individual players, and by the time all eight hands have been completed there will be an astonishing variety of results. Starting out with the same cards, one player may win, another lose; one may go gin while another knocks and is undercut; one may win six points while his neighbor has netted thirty on the hand.

The appeal this has to skilful players is obvious. You can measure yourself against the other players with much greater accuracy when you are playing from exactly the same deal. You may discover that you're not getting as many points out of your winning hands as are possible. You may find out that you're going for gin too often and losing, while other players are steadily accumulating points with the same cards by playing more carefully and knocking when they have the chance. You may even find out that you're better than you thought you were when you compare your own results with those of other players.

I do not know that duplicate gin has ever been attempted on any wide scale. I have played it in my own home, and I find it an enormously satisfying way to play the game. It reduces the number of games you are apt to play in an evening, because everybody will want to discuss and compare results at the end of each hand. This comparison can teach you more about yourself as a gin rummy player in an evening than many months of ordinary play.

I know of few better ways to sharpen your gin wits than duplicate gin. Try it for a while, and before long you'll find that your entire group is playing on a higher level.

Various words are used to describe the three or more card arrangements that can be laid down as matched cards in gin rummy.

OFFICIAL GIN RUMMY SCORE PAD
GAME: 200 POINTS

Scoring During Game

After each hand, winner's score is placed in box; each extra box indicated by X in separate box.
Gin: 25 point bonus plus 2 extra boxes.
Undercut: 25 point bonus plus 1 extra box.

Scoring After Game

Game bonus: 200 points.
Winner gets difference between his game score and opponent's.
Each player gets 25 points for each box.
Schneider (loser is scoreless): Double final score.

PLAYER	PLAYER	PLAYER	PLAYER	PLAYER	PLAYER

Knock Cards

Post-Game Figuring

Winning at Gin

Some of the most common are meld, set, sequence, spread, and run. Run or sequence are used in a more limited way to describe three or more cards of one suit in unbroken sequence.

The type of score pad I recommend is illustrated on the preceding page. This score pad has two special features which I believe add greatly to the convenience of the players. It provides boxes for recording the up card for each hand, and there is space at the bottom for figuring the score at the end of the game.

A Two Hundred Point Game

8

In earlier chapters I have given you pointers on playing technique. These are hard and fast commandments that should be memorized and applied when the situation arises. However, mere absorption is insufficient.

In gin rummy, as in every other skill-luck game, it's one thing to learn a general rule and still another to cope with it in actual play. Like two sets of fingerprints, no two games exactly correspond. A vast network of different situations can arise.

Therefore how do you apply your knowledge?

No man masters his craft without intensive work. It's the same in gin except that we substitute the word "play" for work. Play . . . play . . . play is the answer. Learn by trial and error. In the following pages I'm going to spell out for you a complete 200 point game which I played for the purpose of illustrating my approach in actual practice.

You the reader are a spectator, allowed to kibitz behind my chair.

The game I played, and which I will set forth for you hand by hand and card by card, encompasses many of the points discussed earlier, abetted by a variety of new twists. In some ways this game was "typical," in other ways unorthodox. It was completed in sixteen hands, considered average.

Three hands ended in gin, which is slightly above normal if good-to-expert players are involved. There was one hand that was forced to go to gin (in other words, had an Ace for the turned up card). None of the hands went through the entire deck, although one came dangerously close to it—and I will explain what would have happened if that had occurred.

By no means all the situations that might crop up in a gin game were present. But a great variety of choices presented themselves, and I believe that in a careful study of the following pages you will absorb more faster and retain it longer than you would by committing to memory a hundred pages of rules or abstract discussion of technique.

For this 200 point game I picked a player who had an excellent reputation for skill, but one I had never played before. After the first three or four games I felt I had discovered his method of play (he was much less conservative than I was); before the finish of the first hand I detected how he arranged his cards (in order of face value . . . starting at the right with the low value cards).

At the conclusion of the chapter I will make a few general observations about this contest. If the game had been part of tournament play, in some instances I might have handled my hands differently. Tournament play is a very special situation, and even the outstanding competitors sometimes abandon tournament discipline in ordinary play. In a few specific cases I will explain how I might have made a different move had I been participating in tournament play.

One final suggestion: As you follow the progress of each hand, you might find it helpful to use your own deck of cards and set up the cards corresponding to the ones dealt to me. Then, you can physically make the picks and discards as I make them. In this way you will be holding the same cards that I am at any given point in the game. You might find it interesting to decide what move *you* would make before reading what I did.

Hand One

The cards are shuffled and the draw is made for deal. My opponent draws a six and I draw an Ace, so I deal (low card deals, and in gin rummy the Ace is always low).

After dealing ten cards each to my opponent and myself in rotation, I turn up the next card which is the Jack of spades. This means that the knock can be 10 or less.

I have listed the cards as they fall into meld or meld possibilities, and in order of card value. Actually I do not arrange my hand this way, and as you improve your game to the stage where you can tell at a glance what you hold in your hand regardless of the order of the cards, I suggest that you mix the cards in various positions so that your opponent will be unable to "read" your cards by their placement in your hand. In this instance, I make the following initial arrangement of my cards (as the game progresses, I will shift the arrangement periodically to keep my opponent off balance):

My opponent has first option to pick up the knock card (the turned-up Jack of spades). He refuses it, and I do likewise.

Picking from the deck, my opponent throws the King of hearts, which I refuse.

I pull the King of clubs from the deck and place it at random in my hand. I always do this even if I am going to discard the card I have drawn. Then I shuffle my cards around a bit so my opponent will not know where the card I drew is placed.

In this instance, I throw the card I drew (King of clubs). The average inexperienced player would have held the King of clubs in anticipation of getting King-Queen-Jack of clubs, and would have thrown the 6 of hearts or 3 of clubs instead. At this point, both of those cards are "wild" cards—that is, they don't fit into any meld possibility then existing in my hand. What these players overlook is, at this early part of the game you don't know what cards your opponent is holding, and he may be about to put that 6 or 3 to good use. The King of clubs, on the other hand, is protected, because I am holding the Queen of clubs which arbitrarily rules out a King-Queen-Jack of clubs run and my opponent threw the King of hearts on the previous play—so there is no three-King spread to fear.

As you will readily see, the very next play justified this discard when my Queens shaped up into a spread. Had I not already done so, the logical play at this point would have been to discard the King of clubs. But I am ahead of the inexperienced player in that I have not given up a wild card in the meantime.

My opponent draws from the deck and discards the 8 of hearts. I refuse it. I draw the Queen of spades, giving me a spread of three Queens. My discard is now the Jack of hearts. By throwing the Jack of hearts, you can see that I am breaking the possibility of getting the 9-10-Jack of hearts.

But at this point, I still want to avoid throwing a wild card, and with a Jack sitting in the discard pile, as well as the King of hearts, there is slight chance that my opponent will be able to use the Jack of hearts. If by chance he does use it, I will have the 9 of hearts to use as a layoff.

Negligible as this chance is, let us assume that my opponent has the Queen and 10 of hearts. My Jack of hearts gives him a Queen-Jack-10 run. His advantage is less than is first evident, because it ties up his Queen of hearts and precludes his laying it off on my spread later on for a possible undercut.

My opponent refuses the Jack of hearts, draws from the deck, and throws the King of diamonds. I draw from the deck and pull the Ace of hearts. I now throw the 9 of hearts. Two reasons exist for this. The first is that the 9 of hearts is at least partially protected. Since the 8 and Jack of hearts are both on the discard pile, my opponent can only use it in a three-9 combination. Secondly, the 9 is a high value card, and in a knock situation I want to rid myself of as many of these as possible in favor of holding onto low value cards.

My opponent picks up the 9 of hearts and throws the Jack of diamonds, indicating that he already has a combination of two 9s in his hand, one of them the 9 of diamonds matching the Jack of diamonds.

(This play has contributed an important clue to my opponent's method of play. Even though his cards have fallen into place in this instance, I have become aware that he is a decidedly more reckless player than I am, and this knowledge will serve me well as the game progresses. I realize now that early in the game he held the 8 of hearts, 9 of diamonds, a black 9, and the Jack of diamonds. His discard of the 8 of hearts was a dangerous move, because he had no way of knowing whether I could use it. A safer play at that point—despite the fact that everything broke right for him—would have been to discard the Jack of diamonds, a card partially protected.)

By throwing the Jack of diamonds, my opponent has presented me with the opportunity to revise my hand by breaking up my three-Queen spread and making a run of 10-Jack-Queen of diamonds. I could then throw a safe Queen of spades which cannot be used by my opponent because the Jack of spades was the original knock card.

Undoubtedly this is the safest, the most conservative play to make. I might have played it that way in a tournament or if the hand were further down the deck. However, since this is early in the game and I have already perceived that my opponent tends to take gambles, I choose not to play it that tight.

I draw a 7 of clubs from the deck and throw the 10 of diamonds, which is fairly safe.

My opponent picks the 10 of clubs from the deck and discards it. (He discards it rapidly without putting it into his hand first, which informs me about his hand, plus acquainting me further with his style of play.)

I draw the 6 of spades. Up to now I am playing a defensive game. The way the hand has progressed, I must anticipate that my opponent may shortly be in a position to knock. Therefore my strategy is not so much to attempt to put together new melds as to avoid giving my opponent cards he can use, and to keep as low as possible the number of points I will lose should my opponent decide to knock.

In this case I discard the 6 of hearts, which is safer than the 7 of clubs because I am holding another 6 in my hand.

My opponent draws from the deck and throws the 7 of spades.

I draw the King of spades, slide it into my hand, and then throw it out again.

My opponent, on his next draw from the deck, throws the Jack of clubs.

I pull the 7 of diamonds and throw the 6 of spades. This play is slightly unorthodox. At this point, in addition to those cards, my hand holds a three-Queen spread, a three-deuce spread, 7 of clubs, 3 of clubs, and an Ace of hearts. There is still a 7 outstanding, so I have an opportunity to pick it up from the deck (or if my opponent does, the odds favor his discarding it to me). The 6 of spades is pretty well protected, since my opponent refused the last 6 I threw. And should my opponent knock at this point, there will be only one point difference in my loss of points.

My opponent goes to the deck and knocks with 3 points.

His hand contains two spreads: four 9s and four 4s, affording me no layoffs. After melding my queens and deuces, I am left with two 7s, a 3 and an Ace, adding up to 18 points. Deducting his 3 from this, I lose 15 points on the hand and it's my deal.

Reviewing the hand in the post mortem time, it is apparent that if the game had gone longer and I *had* picked up the outstanding 7, enabling me to knock with one (using my 3 as a discard), my opponent would have laid off his deuce and undercut me by equaling my knock of one.

In that case I would have lost 25 points which he would receive as a bonus for undercutting.

Score at the end of the first hand:

Wander	0
Opponent	15

OFFICIAL GIN RUMMY SCORE PAD
GAME: 200 POINTS

Scoring During Game

After each hand, winner's score is placed in box; each extra box indicated by X in separate box.
Gin: 25 point bonus plus 2 extra boxes.
Undercut: 25 point bonus plus 1 extra box.

Scoring After Game

Game bonus: 200 points.
Winner gets difference between his game score and opponent's.
Each player gets 25 points for each box.
Schneider (loser is scoreless): Double final score.

PLAYER Wander	PLAYER Opponent	PLAYER	PLAYER	PLAYER	PLAYER
	15				

Knock Cards

10															

Post-Game Figuring

A Two Hundred Point Game

Hand Two

Since I lost the last hand, I deal the new one. The knock card in this hand is the 5 of spades. My opponent picks it up. I hold the following cards:

Due to the low knock card—5—you will note some change in the play of the hand.

For his opening play, my opponent throws the King of spades. I draw the 8 of diamonds from the deck and discard the King of diamonds. At this spot it is obvious that the only possibility my opponent has of using the King of diamonds would be in a run of King-Queen-Jack of diamonds.

My opponent draws from the deck, and discards the Jack of diamonds.

I next draw the 3 of clubs from the deck, and my discard is the Jack of clubs. You will note that at this point my discards are relatively safe plays (the Jack of clubs is dead as far as Jacks are concerned and could only be used in a club run).

My opponent draws from the deck and throws the Queen of hearts. I draw the Jack of spades, place it in my hand, and then discard it. Here I could have altered my hand, keeping a 9-10-Jack of spades run and throwing a 10. However, the 10 would be a wild card, whereas I know the Jack of spades cannot possibly be used by my opponent. Two Jacks have already fallen into the discard pile, and the discarded King of spades plus the 10 of spades I am holding rule out a spade run.

Drawing from the deck, my opponent discards the 9 of clubs. I draw the King of clubs from the deck and, after placing it in my hand, throw it into the discard pile. A careless player at this moment might have automatically discarded the 9 of spades, since the top card on the discard pile was another 9. However, if the other player is holding the 7 and 8 of spades, he has walked right into disaster.

A mistake of this type can spell the difference between winning and losing the hand. The King of clubs, on the other hand, is an absolutely dead card.

My opponent draws from the deck, discarding the 8 of hearts. I draw a 2 of spades from the deck and now discard the 9 of spades, which is the safest throw in my hand now that the King of clubs has been discarded.

My opponent refuses the 9 of spades, draws the 7 of spades from the deck, and discards it without putting it into his hand.

I draw the 4 of clubs, which I can use either in a 3-4-5 club run or in a spread of three 4s. I throw the 8 of diamonds, which is as safe as any discard possibility I am holding because there is already one 8 in the discards.

Some players might be tempted to throw the 2 of spades, figuring that they are holding a choice of 3-4-5 of clubs or three 4s; and depending on which they use, both the 5 of clubs and the 4 of spades appear to be good layoff cards. (Remember, my opponent picked up the 5 of spades at the beginning of the hand.) However, the fact should not be ignored that the 2 of spades offers fine possibilities for additional melds, and its low face value is of prime importance in a low knock hand. On the other hand, discarding the 8 of diamonds can give my opponent at best a three card run, since I hold the 10 and 6 of diamonds, and the 6 of diamonds would in that case serve as a layoff.

My opponent draws a 9 of hearts and throws it. I pull the 2 of hearts from the deck.

The 6 of diamonds in my hand matches nothing, and many players would consider it an automatic discard. In terms of my hand this seems easy to excuse. If you drop the 6 of diamonds, there's a chance the other player will drop a 6 of clubs on top of it as a "safe play" which you can then pick up and add to your 3-4-5 club run. This is where the non-alert player makes the error of *playing his own hand only and not his opponent's as well.*

A Two Hundred Point Game   **83**

Study the previous steps in the hand and you will realize that Kings, Jacks, 10s, 9s, 8s, 4s, 3s, and 2s either are dead or have little chance of developing into any profitable combinations for the other player. Chances are he is depending on Aces, 6s, and perhaps 7s to fill his hand. Regarded in that light, the 6 of diamonds becomes a dangerous throw. I discard instead the 4 of hearts, which commits me to my 3-4-5 club run. My opponent can use the 4 of hearts only in a run, which makes my 2 of hearts a good layoff card.

My opponent draws from the deck and discards the 4 of diamonds. Aha! you are saying, if you had discarded the 6 of diamonds on the last play, you would now have a spread of three 4s. This is a long shot. My opponent may have been holding the 4 of diamonds for some time, and may finally have thrown it only *because* I had thrown the 4 of hearts.

I draw the 7 of spades. This discloses that since I also hold the 4 of spades, my opponent must have been filling in a spread of 5s when he picked up the original 5 of spades knock card. If he had established himself as a conservative player, there would be no question in my mind that the 4 of spades is a safe discard. Since I have already seen evidence that my opponent is a speculative player, I dwell upon this before making a decision. I could discard the 6 of diamonds or the 7 of spades, both of which are wild cards, but I might be lucky enough to snare a matching card to the 2 of hearts, 2 of spades, 4 of spades that I hold (either a third deuce or the 3 of spades).

In the end, I make the percentage play and discard the 4 of spades.

My opponent promptly picks up the 4 of spades and discards the deuce of diamonds. I pick up the deuce of diamonds and choose to discard the 7 of spades rather than the 6 of diamonds. If my opponent picked up the 6 to make three 6s, it would eliminate the possibility of his discarding the 6 of clubs to add to my 3-4-5 run. On the other hand, it is now obvious that my opponent has a run in spades. Whether it is 3-4-5, 4-5-6, or 3-4-5-6 I'm not certain. My 7 of spades may add to the sequence. Yet I would rather give him one additional card to an existing run than risk handing him a spread of 6s independent of his 3-4-5 spade run.

My opponent refuses the 7 of spades and discards the 3 of hearts. If I were playing an ordinary player, my next move would not necessitate any hestitation. I would automatically take the 3 of hearts and knock. The cards I hold at this point are:

However, knowing my opponent to be a capable player causes me to question this move before committing myself. So, recognizing his skill, I reason that he *did* have a spread of three 5's to start with, and broke it up for a spade run. This would be sensible only if the run improved his situation because it was a four card meld —in other words, 3-4-5-6 of spades. Actually I would not have to be a genius to figure my opponent's 3-4-5-6 of spades run when he threw the 3 of hearts into the discard.

Why, then, you may wonder, did he refuse my 7 of spades? The answer is that a five card run would be valueless to him if he is going for gin.

Since I have decided that my opponent holds a four- and a three-card meld, it follows that he must have three remaining unmatched cards. This means the danger of my being undercut is negligible, so I pick up the 3 of hearts, turn the 6 of diamonds face down on the discard pile, and knock with 3.

My opponent's melds are the 3-4-5-6 of spades and a spread of three aces. His three unmatched cards are the 5 of diamonds, 5 of hearts, and 6 of hearts, totaling 16 points. Thus I win 13 points on the hand.

In this hand my opponent's strategy, as well as mine, was affected by the fact that we had a comparatively low knock card. My hand could easily have been ginned with the addition of one more card to any of my three melds. My opponent was trying for gin.

A Two Hundred Point Game

You may be curious to know why it was obvious to me that he had a four-card and a three-card meld, leaving him with three unmatched cards. My reasoning was that if he already held a four-card meld in his hand, he would not have picked up the 4 of spades to make another one, which would have given him two odd cards and cut his chances for gin down considerably.

Returning to my opponent's last play, he was at that juncture holding the following cards:

Had he discarded the 5 of diamonds or the 6 of hearts, his chances of gin would have been reduced. Please note that if I had thrown the 6 of diamonds, my opponent could have picked it up for a spread of three 6s and been able to knock with three points. This would leave me holding an unmatched 7 of spades which I could not lay off, and I would have lost four points. Peculiarly, my opponent would have had *two* ways to knock— by using his three 5s, which would be preferable, or the 3-4-5 of spades. But the latter would have meant knocking with five points.

Score at the end of the second hand:

Wander	13
Opponent	15

Winning at Gin

OFFICIAL GIN RUMMY SCORE PAD
GAME: 200 POINTS

Scoring During Game

After each hand, winner's score is placed in box; each extra box indicated by X in separate box.
Gin: 25 point bonus plus 2 extra boxes.
Undercut: 25 point bonus plus 1 extra box.

Scoring After Game

Game bonus: 200 points.
Winner gets difference between his game score and opponent's.
Each player gets 25 points for each box.
Schneider (loser is scoreless): Double final score.

PLAYER Wander	PLAYER Opponent	PLAYER	PLAYER	PLAYER	PLAYER
13	15				

Knock Cards

10	5														

Post-Game Figuring

A Two Hundred Point Game 87

Hand Three

My opponent deals, and the knock card is 10 (King of diamonds). My hand is as follows:

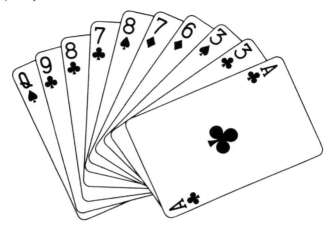

It is immediately apparent that my hand—if the cards run favorably—could shape up into a speedy knock. (At the end of the hand I will explain how the hand could conceivably have been knocked in two plays. Or do you see it for yourself?)

I refuse the knock card, the King of diamonds. My opponent takes it and discards the 10 of spades.

I draw the 5 of hearts from the deck. Since I am already using the 8 of clubs in my hand in a run, I throw the 8 of spades. There exists still another valid reason for discarding the 8 of spades: I am using it as a "fisherman," that is, a card thrown in hope of getting back a card that you need. In this case I am after the 8 of diamonds to make a 6-7-8 run, and my opponent might figure it is safe for him to throw an 8 because there is already one in the discards.

My opponent refuses the 8 of spades, draws from the deck and discards an 8 of hearts. (He reasons as I had hoped he would, even though unfortunately he did not give me the suit I needed.)

I draw the Ace of diamonds from the deck. Average players would unanimously agree as to what card represents the best discard at this point: the Queen of spades. I consider throwing the 7 of diamonds instead, which is a much safer play. If this 200 point game were in its final stages, chances are I would select the

7 of diamonds to discard. However, since neither of us has yet accumulated many points, I make a less cautious play and discard the Queen of spades. Both it and the 5 of hearts I am holding are wild cards, but the 5 is wilder and lower. The fact that my opponent has already picked up a King decreases the chances that the Queen will interest him.

Even if you play conservatively, there are instances when you are forced to choose between taking a risk or playing it too safe and thereby deadening your own hand.

As it turns out, my worries are well founded. My opponent takes the Queen of spades. Wild cards are easily snapped up, and once the gamble is made, don't be surprised when this happens.

My opponent discards the 2 of hearts.

There are many times when I might pick up that 2 of hearts, but in this situation I refuse it as an unnecessarily conservative play. As it turns out, my draw from the deck gives me an additional meld. There was no guarantee that this would happen, but if you play the percentages you will find yourself picking up more and more of these advantages.

I draw the Ace of spades from the deck and now discard the 7 of diamonds. I have an opportunity here to fish for the 5 of diamonds with my five of hearts, but I decide on the safer card.

My opponent refuses the 7 of diamonds. He pulls a 6 from the deck for three 6s, and knocks with 4 points. His melds are three Kings, three Queens, and three 6s, with an unmatched 4.

I lay down my two melds of 7-8-9 of clubs and three Aces, lay off my 6 of diamonds on his three 6s, and—as I have the 3 of clubs, 3 of spades and 5 of hearts left—I take a loss in this hand of 7 points.

You will observe that even though my opponent took the knock card, and in his next three plays picked up a wild Queen and drew a 6 from the deck, he was still able to win only 7 points.

Retracing to my evaluation of my cards at the onset of this hand, I saw that if I had picked up the 5 or 8 of diamonds to complete my diamond run (discarding the 8 of spades) and then picked up either an Ace, deuce, or 3 (discarding the Queen of spades), the Ace or deuce would have given me an 8 or 9 knock and the 3 an additional spread for a one point knock after only two plays.

As it turned out, my diamond run failed to fill in, but I picked up a spread of Aces. This is something to stamp in your mind, particularly in the early stages of any hand: Hands have a way of filling in, one way or another; if they fail to materialize as you originally hoped, they may still come through in another manner. By keeping your strategy flexible and learning to roll with the punches, you can keep the hand working for you rather than slavishly trying to force it into a specific pattern.

Now, after three hands, the cards are running nicely for my opponent. He has picked up the knock card in two of the three hands, and although his throws have generally been on the reckless side, his gambles have mostly paid off. Many a player in my position would be tempted to throw caution to the wind and switch to more offensive maneuvers. But intuition and experience beckon me to stick to my careful play. Things have a way of evening themselves out as the game progresses.

Score at the end of the third hand:

Wander	13
Opponent	22

OFFICIAL GIN RUMMY SCORE PAD
GAME: 200 POINTS

Scoring During Game

After each hand, winner's score is placed in box; each extra box indicated by X in separate box.
Gin: 25 point bonus plus 2 extra boxes.
Undercut: 25 point bonus plus 1 extra box.

Scoring After Game

Game bonus: 200 points.
Winner gets difference between his game score and opponent's.
Each player gets 25 points for each box.
Schneider (loser is scoreless): Double final score.

PLAYER Wander	PLAYER Opponent	PLAYER	PLAYER	PLAYER	PLAYER
13	15				
	22				

Knock Cards

10	5	10															

Post-Game Figuring

A Two Hundred Point Game

Hand Four

I deal the hand, and the knock card is the 8 of diamonds. My hand is as follows:

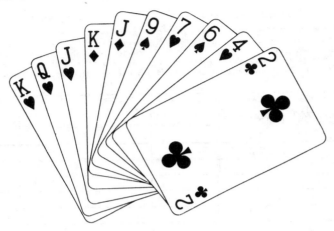

My opponent picks up the knock card and throws the 9 of diamonds, which normally suggests that he is filling in a spread of 8s. However, my first thought is that he may be using his 9 as a fisherman, seeking another 9 to be used in a run.

I draw the 7 of clubs from the deck and discard the King of diamonds, which is virtually dead. My cards are poor ones for a high knock hand, and I want to break away from high value cards having little chance of developing into melds.

My opponent picks from the deck and throws—the Queen of diamonds! Whether he would have thrown it except on top of my King of diamonds is something I have no way of knowing. In any case, it does not alter the fact that my reasoning was sound on my previous play, and I do not dwell on what might have been but turn my mind to future plays.

I draw the 6 of hearts from the deck. My discard is the Jack of diamonds. In two plays I have filled in my hand with matching cards.

But to no avail. Although the Jack of diamonds was a reasonably safe throw, my opponent picks it up for a spread of Jacks. He also holds three 8s, and knocks with 6.

I have only my King-Queen-Jack of hearts to meld, and no layoffs, so my opponent picks up a net of 35 points on the hand.

Winning at Gin

Dropping back to the beginning of the hand, when I speculated that my opponent was fishing for a 9 to fit into a run, it may now appear to you that my reasoning was off base. Not so. When my opponent knocked, his turn-down card was a 10. In other words he was holding two Jacks and a 10 matching one of the Jacks in suit. He could have completed his meld with *either* a 9 to make a run or a Jack to make a spread. Had I given him the 9 he needed, he would have completed his meld two plays earlier.

To date, the cards are running strongly against me and I must play cautiously and try to turn the tide.

Score at the end of the fourth hand:

Wander	13
Opponent	57

OFFICIAL GIN RUMMY SCORE PAD
GAME: 200 POINTS

Scoring During Game

After each hand, winner's score is placed in box; each extra box indicated by X in separate box.
Gin: 25 point bonus plus 2 extra boxes.
Undercut: 25 point bonus plus 1 extra box.

Scoring After Game

Game bonus: 200 points.
Winner gets difference between his game score and opponent's.
Each player gets 25 points for each box.
Schneider (loser is scoreless): Double final score.

PLAYER	PLAYER	PLAYER	PLAYER	PLAYER	PLAYER
Wander	Opponent				
13	15				
	22				
	57				

Knock Cards

10	5	10	8												

Post-Game Figuring

Winning at Gin

Hand Five

Since I lost the last hand, it is my deal and I turn up a knock card of the 9 of clubs. I hold the following cards:

My opponent refuses the knock card, and I pick it up. I am hopeful of a quick knock and I discard the 8 of spades, fully aware that this is a gamble since it is a wild card. If we were playing a 100 point game, I would hesitate to make this move with my opponent already holding 57 points and would instead discard the 4 of diamonds. However, I decide that it is a good gamble, since the unmatched cards in my hand are all low value and should everything go wrong I don't stand to lose many points.

My opponent picks up the 8 of spades (my just reward for a wild play) and discards the King of diamonds. I pick the Queen of diamonds from the deck and, after moving it around in my hand, discard it.

My opponent discards the 10 of spades after picking it from the deck. I pick the 10 of hearts from the deck and throw it.

My opponent picks up the 10 of hearts and knocks with 8-9-10 of hearts, 6-7-8 of spades, and a total of 9 unmatched points. Deducting this from my unmatched 16 points, he picks up a net of 7 points on the hand.

You may question whether I would have put the 10 of hearts on top of my opponent's 10 of spades discard if his 10 of spades had come from his hand rather than from the deck. Or would I have seen it as a fisherman. The answer is that I probably would have discarded it anyway, since I was holding yet another 10 in my hand which made the 10 of hearts appear safe (besides being a high value card). In this particular case the deck provided my opponent with a convenient fisherman, and he didn't have to think twice to seize advantage of it.

I want to emphasize again that I played this hand more vigorously than I would have in tournament or high stakes action. Under those conditions, my opponent would never have had an opportunity to pick up my 8 of spades at the start of the game. The hand could easily have been mine, since several possibilities loomed for a quick knock, and under the circumstances I decided to take that chance. For the purposes of this book, it is probably just as well that I lost, because it illustrates in practice what I have been mentioning in principle: The more you rely on gambles rather than on playing percentages, the more pitfalls await you in the long run.

Score at the end of the fifth hand:

Wander	13
Opponent	64

OFFICIAL GIN RUMMY SCORE PAD
GAME: 200 POINTS

Scoring During Game

After each hand, winner's score is placed in box; each extra box indicated by X in separate box.
Gin: 25 point bonus plus 2 extra boxes.
Undercut: 25 point bonus plus 1 extra box.

Scoring After Game

Game bonus: 200 points.
Winner gets difference between his game score and opponent's.
Each player gets 25 points for each box.
Schneider (loser is scoreless): Double final score.

PLAYER Wander	PLAYER Opponent	PLAYER	PLAYER	PLAYER	PLAYER
13	15				
	22				
	57				
	64				

Knock Cards

10	5	10	8	9											

Post-Game Figuring

A Two Hundred Point Game

Hand Six

I deal, and the knock card is 10 (King of hearts). My hand is the following:

Neither player uses the King of hearts. My opponent draws from the deck and discards the Jack of spades, which I pick up. My discard is the Jack of hearts, a good percentage play because I hold two other Jacks in my hand; and if my opponent should use it in a run (which would have to be 10-Jack-Queen, since the King is out), my Queen of clubs would become a safe discard and I could lay off my 9 of hearts on his meld.

The average player would have thrown the Queen of clubs, 6 of diamonds, or 4 of spades, holding onto the Jack and 9 of hearts in hope of picking up the 10 of hearts. In terms of percentages, any of those plays would have been riskier.

I stress this even though the play backfired: My opponent picks up the Jack of hearts. He in turn discards the 6 of clubs.

I draw the Jack of clubs from the deck. This affords me an opportunity to rearrange my hand into three 9s and three jacks, giving me two 10s along with my Queen of clubs which are safe discards.

I throw the Queen of clubs.

Regarding this last play, in retrospect I believe a superior play would have been to discard one of the 10s. The Queen of clubs was reasonably well protected, since my opponent was holding a 10-Jack-Queen run in hearts and chances were slender that he would be holding the two remaining Queens. The 10s, however, were even better protected, since I had a pair of them and had nines and Jacks on either sides of them. (Even so, they were not completely dead: If my opponent held three Queens, Jack of hearts, 10 of hearts, and another 10, my 10 would enable him to shift his hand to three Queens and three 10s.)

But this possibility is so remote that, in reviewing the hand, I prefer the 10 discard over the Queen. As it turned out, my opponent was unable to use either card. I cite this as an instance of how simple it is to pass up the best possible play. At times such lapses can prove costly.

My hand is now arranged as follows:

The Queen of clubs is refused, and my opponent after drawing from the deck discards the 5 of spades. I draw the 5 of diamonds from the deck, discarding the 10 of diamonds.

My opponent draws from the deck and discards the King of spades. I draw the 4 of clubs from the deck and discard the 10 of spades.

My opponent picks the 8 of spades from the deck and throws it on the discard pile without placing it in his hand. I draw the 7 of clubs from the deck and now discard the 6 of diamonds.

You see that I have broken away from the 5-6 of diamonds in order to avoid throwing the 7 of clubs. There is already a 6 in the discards, and my 5 and 9 of diamonds would prevent my opponent from using it for more than a three-card run, on which I could lay off my 5. The 7 of clubs, on the other hand, is totally unprotected.

My opponent draws from the deck and knocks with 3 points. His melds are 10-Jack-Queen of hearts, three Aces, and three deuces. I have no layoffs and have 20 losing points in my hand (7 of clubs, 5 of diamonds, 4 of clubs, 4 of spades). My net loss on the hand is 17 points.

I am still scrambling and striving to break my opponent's run of cards.

Score at the end of the sixth hand.

Wander	13
Opponent	81

Chester Wander
International Gin Rummy Champion

OFFICIAL GIN RUMMY SCORE PAD
GAME: 200 POINTS

Scoring During Game

After each hand, winner's score is placed in box; each extra box indicated by X in separate box.
Gin: 25 point bonus plus 2 extra boxes.
Undercut: 25 point bonus plus 1 extra box.

Scoring After Game

Game bonus: 200 points.
Winner gets difference between his game score and opponent's.
Each player gets 25 points for each box.
Schneider (loser is scoreless): Double final score.

PLAYER Wander	PLAYER Opponent	PLAYER	PLAYER	PLAYER	PLAYER
13	15				
	22				
	57				
	64				
	81				

Knock Cards

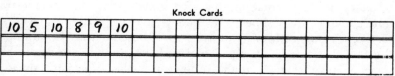

10	5	10	8	9	10											

Post-Game Figuring

A Two Hundred Point Game

Hand Seven

I deal the cards, and the turn-up card is the Ace of clubs. This makes it mandatory that the hand be played to gin. My hand is as follows:

Both players refuse the turn-up card. If this had been a high knock game, I might have picked up the Ace of clubs because of its possible future value as a knock card. However, this is a gin hand, and my refusal of the Ace (after my opponent had refused it) has a built-in advantage for me. It serves as a fisherman, since my opponent—assuming I had no interest in Aces— might drop the Ace of spades on the discard pile.

My opponent draws first and his discard is the 4 of spades, which I of course take. My discard is the Queen of diamonds. This is the discard the average player would make, but if you have been following my style of play carefully, you will realize that it is a surprising play for me.

Let me assure you that I do not consider it the best discard to make in this situation, but occasionally for this demonstration game I will deliberately render "average player" moves so that you, along with me, can assess the consequences. In addition, the fact that this hand is to be played for gin calls for somewhat stronger play than I might ordinarily make—especially since I already possess two melds in my hand and I know I am playing against a player who generally is on the offensive.

My normal choice of discard here would have been one of the Kings. It may appear odd to break up a pair of Kings in a hand already containing two three-card melds, but in tournament play this would unquestionably have been my move.

Again, let me stress what I have repeated earlier in the book: Hands have a way of filling themselves, in one pattern or another, and at this early stage of the hand I would be more concerned (in tournament play) about feeding wild cards to my opponent than about breaking up a pair that might or might not turn into a set. This is particularly true when the cards involved are of high face value.

The Queen of diamonds is picked up by my opponent (the lesson is clear). He discards the Jack of clubs. I have no way of knowing whether he has used the Queen of diamonds in a spread of Queens or as part of a run and, if it is a run, whether it is King-Queen-Jack of diamonds or Queen-Jack-10. Should the run involve the King, I not only have given my opponent a useful card but have enabled him to tie up one of the two Kings that are unaccounted for. If, on the other hand, I had thrown a King, chances are it would have been useless to him; and even if I had thrown the Queen of diamonds later on, it's probable that by then his hand would have shaped up differently and it would no longer have been of any use to him. He most likely would have followed my lead and discarded his King as a dead card.

I am detailing these possibilities to demonstrate the far-reaching effects a single play can have on the outcome of a hand.

I pick the Jack of spades from the deck and, after placing it in my hand, discard it. Do you understand why this play would be made at this time?

My opponent discards the 8 of clubs after making a pick from the deck. I draw the 10 of diamonds from the deck. It is clear that if my opponent used the Queen of diamonds in a run, it is King-Queen-Jack. Now that the Jack of clubs rests on the discard pile, it is no longer a question of either King being an equally good discard.

I discard the King of clubs. On the long-shot chance that my opponent will pick it up, I can use his acceptance of it as a valuable source of information. It would reveal that he holds three Kings and three Queens (he would have scant reason to break up a King-Queen-Jack of diamonds run for a set of Kings). His hand would therefore be disclosed to me except for whatever third spread he might be trying for.

My opponent draws from the deck and discards the 6 of spades. I draw the 3 of hearts from the deck. As you can see, it matches my hand very well, and I throw the King of hearts as the proper discard.

My opponent draws from the deck and discards the 7 of clubs. I draw the 2 of hearts from the deck and discard the 8 of hearts. (There is already an 8 on the discard pile. If you remember this without having to refer to earlier paragraphs, you're far along on the road toward developing one of the best assets a gin rummy player can have—a good memory.)

Let me again mention something stated earlier. I strongly recommend that you use a standard gin rummy tray when playing the game. This will act as a deterrent against the temptations to peek at previous discards, which is of course absolutely illegal in gin rummy, although allowed by many players. You will never ascend higher than a plane of mediocrity if you disregard this rule and miss the complete satisfaction achieved by winning a game properly.

My opponent draws from the deck and discards the 3 of diamonds. I pick up the 3 of diamonds and throw the 6 of hearts. The 3 of diamonds furnishes me with increased flexibility in setting the nice layout of 4s, 3s, and 2s, in my hand, which now appears like this:

The 6 of hearts is my best discard because the 8 of hearts has already been discarded, the 4 of hearts is in my hand, and the 6 of spades was thrown earlier by my opponent. The 10 of diamonds, on the other hand, is still a wide open card.

However, my opponent picks up the 6 of hearts and discards the 6 of diamonds. I now know he has the 5-6-7 of hearts.

I draw the King of spades from the deck and, after placing it in my hand, I discard it. My opponent draws the Queen of spades from the deck and discards it. This play, linked with the fact that I have the 10 of diamonds in my hand, pins down another meld in his hand of King-Queen-Jack of diamonds.

I draw the Queen of clubs, then discard it. Note that Kings and Queens have by now become unimportant in this hand except as discards.

My opponent draws from the deck and discards the 9 of clubs. I draw the 2 of diamonds from the deck, which gives me gin, with four 4s, three 3s, three 2s, and my 10 of diamonds as a discard. As my opponent is left with 8 points in his hand, I receive 8 points plus a 25 point bonus for gin, which gives me 33 points, plus two extra boxes—an added bonus for going gin.

My opponent's hand at the conclusion of the game looked like this:

At first glance it appears a hand that is close to the point of gin. All that is required is a fourth card to any of his three melds to do the trick. But what cards would do that for him? The King-

Queen-Jack of diamonds needs the 10, which I have held for half the game. The spread of 10s requires the same card. The 7-6-5 of hearts needs the 4 (the 8 of hearts is in the discards), and I am using the 4 of hearts in a spread of my own. So the hand, set up as it is, is impossible to gin! This did not happen by chance. As already shown, I had analyzed what two of his melds were and knew that they were blocked. I did not know he had a spread of 10s, but I regarded it as a strong possibility based on the cards that had appeared in the game.

At the conclusion of the hand, my opponent and I discussed the hypothetical question of what discard he would have made if he had drawn the 9 of spades into his hand. We both agreed that the wisest discard would have been the 10 of clubs, which was dead. This would have opened up the possibility of picking up the 7 of spades and would have given him a choice of two cards to complete his hand for gin, instead of having to rely on the 10 of diamonds as the fourth card for two different melds. Besides, discard of the 10 of clubs would have enabled him to fish for the outstanding 10 of diamonds.

However, I think the predicament of my opponent's blocked hand originated with plays he made much earlier in the game. Since I wasn't playing the hand, I can't say play by play where the hand went wrong. Still, there is a valuable lesson to be learned, and here are a few pointers to remember:

1. Keep your hand flexible by planning it in a way that will give you the greatest number of possible plays to fill it.

2. Whenever possible, avoid making your hand dependent on blocked melds.

3. Don't become so engrossed in your hand that you forget your opponent's.

In the case of my opponent's hand, I would have broken up the two 10s (using them to fish for the 10 of diamonds) and would have held onto the low value cards he discarded to my good advantage.

This was a lengthy game. Maybe the pattern is broken.

Score at the end of the seventh hand:

Wander	46
Opponent	81

Winning at Gin

OFFICIAL GIN RUMMY SCORE PAD
GAME: 200 POINTS

Scoring During Game

After each hand, winner's score is placed in box; each extra box indicated by X in separate box.
Gin: 25 point bonus plus 2 extra boxes.
Undercut: 25 point bonus plus 1 extra box.

Scoring After Game

Game bonus: 200 points.
Winner gets difference between his game score and opponent's.
Each player gets 25 points for each box.
Schneider (loser is scoreless): Double final score.

PLAYER Wander	PLAYER Opponent	PLAYER	PLAYER	PLAYER	PLAYER
13	15				
46	22				
X	57				
X	64				
	81				

Knock Cards

10	5	10	8	9	10	1									

Post-Game Figuring

A Two Hundred Point Game

Hand Eight

My opponent deals, and the knock card is the deuce of spades. My hand is as follows:

I pick up the knock card, the 2 of spades, and discard the 5 of hearts. The deuce of spades offers meld possibilities in my hand and is also a valuable card to have in a low knock hand. My opponent picks from the deck and discards the King of spades.

I draw the 8 of diamonds from the deck, add it to my 5-6-7 run, and discard the Queen of hearts. Why this card instead of the Jack of diamonds? Both are wild, but if my Jack were to complete a spread for my opponent, this might tie up the Jack of clubs, which would block one end of my possible club run.

My opponent picks from the deck and throws the Queen of diamonds. I pick the 7 of hearts from the deck and discard it after placing it in my hand.

My opponent draws from the deck, uses the card he has drawn, and discards the 7 of spades. I draw the 8 of hearts from the deck and now fish for the 8 of clubs by discarding it. The 8 of hearts is protected by my 8 of diamonds and the discarded 7 of hearts.

My opponent picks the 10 of hearts from the deck and discards it. I draw the 4 of diamonds from the deck, add it to my diamond sequence, and now discard the Jack of diamonds. Before making this move I consider two other possibilities. One is to discard the 10 of clubs, which I reject as "too safe" a play in this hand with its low knock card. The other possibility is the 8 of diamonds. This may surprise you, since the 8 of diamonds is part of a meld, but ordinarily a five-card meld is of little value to a hand. However, with the 9 and 10 of diamonds unaccounted for, this could complete a run for my opponent as easily as the Jack could. So I decide to discard the higher value card.

My opponent picks up the Jack of diamonds. While I have not been playing "tight" according to my standards, my play in this game has been more guarded than most people generally play. Even so, have you noticed the high percentage of times my riskier plays have kicked back on me?

My opponent's discard is the Ace of diamonds, which I take to add to the two Aces in my hand. I discard the 10 of clubs, which probably is a safe card. But should my opponent pick it up, I would have a layoff of the 9 of clubs. Even my deuce offers good possibilities as a layoff, since the majority of the cards that have appeared in the game thus far are high value cards.

My opponent draws from the deck and discards the King of hearts. I draw the 8 of spades from the deck, place it in my hand, and then discard it. My opponent draws the 8 of clubs from the deck and discards it. I draw the 7 of clubs from the deck and discard it. Those last three moves involving 8s and 7s have been practically automatic, since it is obvious both to me and my opponent that these cards are dead.

My opponent draws from the deck and discards the 5 of clubs. I draw the 5 of spades from the deck and discard it. Fives are dead as a spread, and if my opponent should be able to use it in a run, my 2 of spades might fit in as a layoff. On the other hand, no 9s have turned up so far in the game and I suspect strongly that my opponent is looking for one.

My opponent picks up the 5 of spades and throws the 3 of hearts. I draw the 4 of hearts from the deck and discard it. My opponent picks up and discards the 6 of hearts.

I draw the Jack of hearts from the deck and discard it. Even though I know my opponent is holding Jacks, I prefer to give him an addition to his spread rather than a fresh 9 of clubs. When a hand has progressed as far as this one, you must assume that your opponent's hand is pretty well developed. This raises the probability that my Jack of hearts will empower him to go gin. Should this be the case, it follows that even if I avoided making this discard and subsequently I was able to knock, he would probably undercut me and still get a 25 point bonus. For this reason, most good players prefer to take this risk rather than the greater risk of throwing a card that could give the opponent an additional meld and turn a partially developed hand into a gin or knock hand.

Naturally, my opponent picks up the Jack of hearts. His discard is the 6 of clubs. I pick the Queen of spades from the deck and discard it.

My opponent picks from the deck and discards the 9 of spades. This confirms my original judgment that he has been holding two 9s. By holding onto my 9 of clubs, I have forced him to reset his hand so that the 9s are no longer of use to him. Now if the cards run right (and I will do everything I can to cause this to happen) this situation may serve me very well indeed.

I draw the 2 of clubs from the deck and discard the 9 of clubs, which has now become a safe throw. My opponent picks from the deck and, as I had hoped, throws the 9 of diamonds from his hand.

I pick up the 9 of diamonds and knock with 2 points.

Some players might be sorely tempted to let play continue for another few moves in hopes of going gin. This could prove a dangerous, if not disastrous, decision. I know my opponent has 4 Jacks, and I assume he completed another meld. This would leave him with three unmatched cards in his hand. Since I picked up the deuce of spades (the knock card) and later picked up an Ace which my opponent had discarded, it is reasonable to assume that he is holding other cards of those denominations. He certainly would not discard them after I have demonstrated interest in them, and they have obvious usefulness as knock cards and possible layoffs.

My guess is that my opponent is left with three unmatched cards: two 2s and an Ace. This turns out to be the case, and after he lays off his Ace on my Ace spread, I win 2 points on the hand.

Score at the end of the eighth hand:

Wander	48
Opponent	81

OFFICIAL GIN RUMMY SCORE PAD
GAME: 200 POINTS

Scoring During Game

After each hand, winner's score is placed in box; each extra box indicated by X in separate box.
Gin: 25 point bonus plus 2 extra boxes.
Undercut: 25 point bonus plus 1 extra box.

Scoring After Game

Game bonus: 200 points.
Winner gets difference between his game score and opponent's.
Each player gets 25 points for each box.
Schneider (loser is scoreless): Double final score.

PLAYER	PLAYER	PLAYER	PLAYER	PLAYER	PLAYER
Wander	Opponent				
13	15				
46	22				
X	57				
X	64				
48	81				

Knock Cards

10	5	10	8	9	10	1	2								

Post-Game Figuring

A Two Hundred Point Game

Hand Nine

My opponent deals, and the knock card is the 8 of spades.
I hold the following cards:

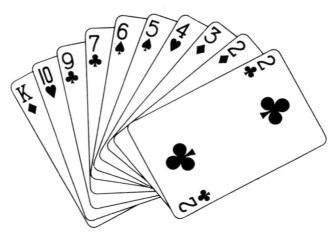

We both pass up the 8 of spades. I draw the 8 of clubs from
the deck, which fills in my spread of the 7-8-9 of clubs. My discard is the King of diamonds. Cards seem to be running my way
now, and I'll open up a bit more offensively. Besides, there is
no high value card in my hand that is protected. Because the
King is at one end of the card spectrum, it can't be used in as
many combinations as the 10 of hearts. Of course the 10 might
be used to fish for the 10 of clubs (and I may do this on the
next play).

My opponent draws from the deck and discards the 7 of spades.
I pick up the 7 of spades, which gives me a second run with my
5 and 6 of spades. I discard the 10 of hearts.

My opponent picks up the 10 of hearts and discards the Jack
of spades. It is now evident that the King was the safer first
discard. I pick the 6 of hearts from the deck and discard it. This
has several advantages as a throw card over the 2 of clubs, which
would be my second choice. I hold the 6 of spades, thus cutting
down the possibilities of my opponent getting three 6s. If he has
a run of hearts, with his 10 of hearts as the high card, my 6 of
hearts would be the fifth card in the meld; and as I have dwelt
upon before, a five-card spread can often prove more of a trap

than an advantage. If, as is more likely, my opponent has filled in a heart run of 5-6-7, then my 4 of hearts becomes a layoff and presents me with the possibility of an undercut. Finally, by discarding the 6, I could knock with the addition of but a single card to one of my melds, or even with the draw of an Ace, which would bring down the total count of my unmatched cards to eight.

My opponent draws from the deck and discards the Queen of diamonds. I draw the 6 of clubs from the deck, which adds to my 7-8-9 run and enables me to knock with 7 (3 of diamonds, 2 of diamonds, and 2 of clubs unmatched).

Since my opponent had just started to break his hand, I catch him with 26 points and win a net of 19 points on the hand.

The lesson contained in this game stands out boldly. Do you see it? I can sum it up in one word: KNOCK. The hand is a beautiful one to play for gin. Here is where temptation can rear its head, whispering in your ear, "Go another two or three plays and then it's gin." Learn to ignore that little voice. The game has moved swiftly, the knock card is a relatively high one, and my opponent's discards have revealed that his hand has not yet jelled. Two or three more plays might find me in exactly the same position I was in at the point where I knocked; but by then the other player could have pulled just the cards needed for him to knock, or undercut me, or conceivably even to go gin.

If you recall one thing only from the contents of this entire book, let it be the following: In nearly all situations, the correct action is to knock at the first occasion. Failure to do so is probably the most common error made by gin rummy players. By remembering this rule, you will not only win more hands but you will gain more points on the hands that you win.

Score at the end of the ninth hand:

Wander	67
Opponent	81

Chester Wander
International Gin Rummy Champion

OFFICIAL GIN RUMMY SCORE PAD
GAME: 200 POINTS

Scoring During Game

After each hand, winner's score is placed in box; each extra box indicated by X in separate box.
Gin: 25 point bonus plus 2 extra boxes.
Undercut: 25 point bonus plus 1 extra box.

Scoring After Game

Game bonus: 200 points.
Winner gets difference between his game score and opponent's.
Each player gets 25 points for each box.
Schneider (loser is scoreless): Double final score.

PLAYER	PLAYER	PLAYER	PLAYER	PLAYER	PLAYER
Wander	Opponent				
13	15				
46	22				
X	57				
X	64				
48	81				
67					

Knock Cards

10	5	10	8	9	10	1	2	8							

Post-Game Figuring

Winning at Gin

Hand Ten

My opponent deals, and the up card is the Jack of diamonds.
My hand is as follows:

I refuse the Jack of diamonds. My opponent picks it up and
discards the Jack of clubs. This play discloses valuable information about my opponent's hand. Do you see what melds he
could have made using the Jack of diamonds—and what spreads
he could not have made? His play also divulges something additional: Since he must be aware that he has provided information
on this play, I assume that he is intent on a quick knock, and
I will gear my own play accordingly.

I draw the Ace of diamonds from the deck and automatically
throw the Jack of spades. The Queen of spades is also a protected card, but it could possibly serve me as a layoff card (should
my opponent meld the 9-10-Jack of spades) whereas the Jack has
no chance of being a layoff.

My opponent draws from the deck and discards the Queen of
hearts. I draw the 5 of clubs from the deck and now discard the
Queen of spades, which has become a dead card because of my
opponent's last discard. Note also that while I have abandoned
the meld possibilities of the Jack-Queen-King of spades on the
last two discards, I have at the same time improved my hand,
because I have new meld possibilities with my two 5s and have
also lowered the total point value of my unmatched cards.

My opponent draws from the deck and discards the 7 of hearts. I draw the 5 of hearts from the deck, making my spread of 5s. (Make that an exclamation point at the end of the last paragraph). Rather than throw a wild 6 of diamonds, I break my 9s. Since the 9 of diamonds could add to my opponent's diamond run if I throw it and provide me with a key layoff if I keep it on either a spread of 9s or a diamond run, I discard the 9 of hearts.

My opponent draws from the deck and discards the 10 of spades. I draw the King of spades from the deck and discard it.

My opponent draws from the deck and discards the 9 of clubs. I draw the 8 of clubs from the deck, and although I realize my opponent may have a diamond run from the 10 up, I would prefer to add to it rather than give him one of the two wilder cards in my hand—the 8 of clubs and 6 of diamonds. Should my opponent use the 9 of diamonds in a new diamond run of 9-8-7, my 6 of diamonds would then be a layoff. I consider the 8 of clubs the least desirable of the three cards to throw, since it offers the greatest number of possibilities to my opponent for fitting it into a meld.

My opponent picks up the 9 of diamonds, a possibility I had anticipated, and discards the 8 of spades. I draw the 3 of spades and discard the now safe (as distinguished from "dead") 8 of clubs.

My opponent draws the 6 of hearts from the deck and discards it. I draw the 7 of clubs from the deck and discard it automatically as a dead card. If you fail to see why, check the previous plays in the hand as well as the cards I am holding and it will become clear why it cannot be used.

My opponent picks the 6 of clubs from the deck and discards it. I draw the 8 of hearts from the deck—a dead card—and discard it.

My opponent draws from the deck and knocks with five points. After laying down my melds (three 5s and three 2s), I have 11 points in unmatched cards: 6 of diamonds, 3 of spades, Ace of diamonds, Ace of hearts. My opponent wins a net of 6 points on the hand.

As I stated at the start of the hand, my opponent's initial play determined my strategy for the game. When it was apparent that he was striving for a fast knock, I decided to play the hand defensively. I accomplished this by ridding myself of high value—

yet safe—cards while trying to fill my hand with low value cards.

But, you may be thinking, my opponent discarded the 10 of spades which would have given me a run with my Jack-Queen. Remember, though, that he threw this card only *after* I had discarded the Jack and Queen, and almost certainly only *because* I had discarded them.

Yes, but what of the fact that I then drew the King of spades from the deck, which would have filled in the spread at the other end? This occurred well into the game, and if I had set my strategy differently—that is, more aggressively—the entire hand would have been altered and there is no way of knowing whether this card would have come to me. Also, if I had thrown wild cards while looking for the King of spades, my opponent might have been able to knock before that point in the game, inflicting a heavier loss on me.

Remember, also, that if I had stuck grimly to the Jack-Queen of spades and the two 9s in my original hand, I would not have made the spread of 5s, etc. and reduced my point count of unmatched cards.

None of these possibilities was worth the risk. I could have been caught with 30 or 40 points instead of losing only 6.

Score at the end of the tenth hand:

| Wander | 67 |
| Opponent | 87 |

Chester Wander
International Gin Rummy Champion

OFFICIAL GIN RUMMY SCORE PAD
GAME: 200 POINTS

Scoring During Game

After each hand, winner's score is placed in box; each extra box indicated by X in separate box.
Gin: 25 point bonus plus 2 extra boxes.
Undercut: 25 point bonus plus 1 extra box.

Scoring After Game

Game bonus: 200 points.
Winner gets difference between his game score and opponent's.
Each player gets 25 points for each box.
Schneider (loser is scoreless): Double final score.

PLAYER	PLAYER	PLAYER	PLAYER	PLAYER	PLAYER
Wander	*Opponent*				
13	15				
46	22				
✗	57				
✗	64				
48	81				
67	87				

Knock Cards

10	5	10	8	9	10	1	2	8	10								

Post-Game Figuring

Winning at Gin

Hand Eleven

I deal, and the knock card is the deuce of diamonds. My hand is as follows:

My opponent having refused the 2 of diamonds, I take it, thereby increasing my diamond run to four cards. In the hand just completed, I decided after my opponent's first play to proceed with caution. In the current hand the situation is somewhat different. Because of the deuce of diamonds knock card the hand has a good chance of going to gin. I have been gaining steadily on my opponent, despite my slight point setback in the hand just played, and I feel percentage is beginning to work in my favor.

I decide on a more offensive technique here. I discard the King of spades instead of the safer (but more useful to my hand) 6 of clubs. I prefer the King discard to the 9 of diamonds for the same reason I discarded a King instead of a 10 as my first throw in Hand No. 9. My decision toward aggressive play is, at this point, tentative. If my opponent picks up the King of spades discard, I may pull in my horns a little.

My opponent picks from the deck and discards the 8 of diamonds. I draw the 6 of diamonds from the deck, giving me a second meld. My discard is the 9 of diamonds. Can you understand why I prefer to hold onto the 7 of hearts? Even though my 6 of hearts is now tied up in a spread of 6s, should a 5 or an 8 of hearts appear I might wish to rearrange my hand as follows: 7-6-5 of hearts, 6-5-4-3 of diamonds, 2 of diamonds, 2 of hearts, Ace of hearts.

A Two Hundred Point Game 119

My opponent picks from the deck and throws the King of diamonds from his hand. I draw the 4 of spades from the deck and discard it as a card that is partially protected by the 4 of diamonds in my hand.

The 4 of spades is not taken. My opponent draws from the deck and discards the Queen of diamonds. I pick the 10 of hearts from the deck and throw it into the discard pile. I am continuing to play this hand strong.

My opponent, after having picked a card from the deck, discards the 6 of spades, which I pick up. By discarding the Ace of hearts instead of the 7 of hearts, I have a four-way instead of a three-way shot at gin. Either of the two outstanding deuces, the 8 of hearts, or the 5 of hearts would turn the trick. If I discarded the 7 of hearts, I would require the 3 of hearts or one of the deuces to go gin—three opportunities instead of four. Even should my opponent be able to use my discard in a spread of Aces, the fact that he has not taken any cards from me up to now leads me to believe that this would not be sufficient to give him gin or place me in a dangerous position; and I am not, of course, in a knocking condition at this time.

My opponent takes the Ace of hearts and discards the 5 of hearts from his hand, which gives me gin.

Due in part, no doubt, to the low knock card, my opponent has played wilder than customary. His hand at the end of the game looked like this:

Winning at Gin

His unmatched cards total 44 points, and adding to this the gin bonus of 25 points, I win 69 points on the hand plus two extra boxes. The type of plays that I have been employing as I go along are based on the play of my opponent as well as on percentage moves. It is necessary to handle your hands in this manner to play winning gin.

Even though my opponent has won 6 games to my five, I am leading.

Score at the end of the eleventh hand:

Wander	136
Opponent	87

Chester Wander
International Gin Rummy Champion

OFFICIAL GIN RUMMY SCORE PAD
GAME: 200 POINTS

Scoring During Game

After each hand, winner's score is placed in box; each extra box indicated by X in separate box.
Gin: 25 point bonus plus 2 extra boxes.
Undercut: 25 point bonus plus 1 extra box.

Scoring After Game

Game bonus: 200 points.
Winner gets difference between his game score and opponent's.
Each player gets 25 points for each box.
Schneider (loser is scoreless): Double final score.

PLAYER	PLAYER	PLAYER	PLAYER	PLAYER	PLAYER
Wander	Opponent				
13	15				
46	22				
X	57				
X	64				
48	81				
67	87				
136					
X					
X					

Knock Cards

10	5	10	8	9	10	1	2	8	10	2						

Post-Game Figuring

Winning at Gin

Hand Twelve

My opponent deals and turns up the 6 of spades for a knocking card. I hold the following hand:

Having first choice, I take the 6 of spades up card into my hand. Since the cards are running better and the knock card is fairly low, I discard the 9 of hearts as a fisherman instead of the more conservative percentage play of the King of diamonds.

My opponent picks from the deck and throws the King of spades. This fortunate turn of events does not alter the fact that the King of diamonds would have been a "safer" discard on my last play—one that under many circumstances I would have made. Perhaps I can best describe my approach to gin rummy by stating that I do not firmly believe in either offensive or defensive play as a matter of general policy. My dogma is conservatism. To me this implies methodically evaluating each existing situation—the hand, the knock card, how the cards are running, the percentages, the style of my opponent, the advisability of making sporadic shifts in play to keep my opponent guessing, and the numerous other factors that go into a game, including even intuition—and basing my play on that evaluation.

Naturally I pick up the King of spades, and I now discard the Jack of spades. The 10 of clubs is a safer discard, but again I am playing this hand according to the run of the cards.

My opponent picks from the deck and discards the Jack of diamonds.

I draw the 2 of clubs from the deck and wait no longer to break up my 8 of diamonds, 10 of diamonds, 10 of clubs combination. I discard the 10 of clubs. My opponent draws from the deck and discards the 10 of hearts from his hand.

I draw the Ace of diamonds from the deck and discard a safe 10 of diamonds. My hand now shapes up like this:

It doesn't look very impressive. But I am not in the least worried by my four totally unmatched cards. Just a couple of plays can change the picture. Let's see what happens.

My opponent draws the 9 of diamonds from the deck and discards it. I draw the Jack of clubs from the deck and discard it. Although I haven't mentioned it in every instance, you can always assume that any card I draw from the deck is not discarded until I have first placed it in my hand and moved it around a bit. My opponent's last discard, on the other hand, was obviously the card he had just picked.

My opponent draws the 9 of clubs from the deck and discards it. I draw the Ace of clubs from the deck and discard the 8 of diamonds. Now, just two moves after the situation shown in the last diagram, I have rid myself of the high value and useless 8 of diamonds and reduced my unmatched cards to a total of 8 points; and I still have a choice of one of three cards for a new meld (3 of clubs, Ace of hearts, Ace of spades). In addition, I am in a good position for a knock or undercut.

Winning at Gin

My opponent picks from the deck and discards the 8 of spades. I pick the 7 of spades from the deck and discard it.

My opponent picks up my 7 of spades discard and throws the 4 of spades. This contains no element of surprise. In considering my previous discard, I realized that both the 7 of spades and the 4 of diamonds were not without risk as discards, but nothing in my opponent's play indicates that he is yet in a situation to knock, and if he should I occupy an excellent position for an undercut.

I draw the 8 of hearts from the deck and then discard it. My opponent draws the Queen of hearts from the deck and discards it.

I draw the Queen of clubs from the deck and throw it into the discards. My opponent draws from the deck and discards the 4 of spades, I draw the 4 of clubs from the deck and discard the 4 of diamonds.

Why this choice?

The 3-5-6 of clubs are out, and the 2-3-5 of diamonds are out, so either of the 4s can be used in a spread. If my opponent makes a club spread, my Ace and deuce could be laid off on it. If he makes a diamond spread, I have only my Ace to lay off on it. On the other hand, if I keep the 4 of diamonds and then draw the 3 of clubs to make a meld I can only knock, whereas if I keep the 4 of clubs and get the 3 of clubs I can go gin. All of these factors are carefully weighed before I arrive at my final decision to discard the diamond.

The 4 of diamonds is picked up by my opponent, who discards the 5 of hearts. I pick the 5 of spades from the deck and discard it. My opponent draws from the deck and discards the 9 of spades. I draw the Queen of spades from the deck and discard it. My opponent discards the 2 of spades after picking it from the deck.

I could now pick up the 2 of spades from the discard pile and knock with six points. But we are almost to the bottom of the deck, and before deciding I analyze the situation. I know my opponent has a spread of 7s, also a run of diamonds (2-3-4, 3-4-5, or 2-3-4-5). What of the rest of his hand? Based on the cards that have already appeared in the game, the only other meld he could possibly have is a spread of 3s, and this is a remote chance, since he has one 3 tied up in his diamond spread. The fact that he discarded the 4 of hearts rules out his having the Ace-2-3 of hearts.

His discard of the 2 of spades makes either Ace-2-3 of spades or a spread of 2s impossible. If he has the spread of 3s, he would almost surely be in a knocking position, since he would have only one unmatched card and chances are it would be of low value. Further, he knows that I have Kings and 6s, and he could be holding either or both of these as layoffs.

This is the way I analyze the situation: (1) It seems to me that he has a hand that is nearly impossible to gin; (2) If I knock, I would most likely be undercut and give my opponent a bonus of 25 points; (3) If my opponent knocks, at worst I have very little to lose in unmatched points: (4) At this point, there is a strong possibility that the hand will go to the bottom of the deck and end scoreless for either of us. Weighing all these factors, I decide not to knock.

I have gone into this lengthy analysis for a definite reason—to underscore the vital importance to a good gin rummy player of remembering the cards that have been played. If I had not disciplined my memory through many years of practice, I would have been unable to perceive that my usual rule of "knock at the first opportunity" would in this case be a grave mistake.

I draw the Jack of hearts from the deck and discard it. My opponent draws and discards the 3 of clubs. I pick it up for gin.

Let's take a look at my opponent's hand. He was sitting there with these cards:

Had I knocked with 6 when the opportunity presented itself

Winning at Gin

a few plays back, my opponent would have laid off the King of clubs and the 6 of clubs on my melds and undercut me.

Now examine his last discard—the 3 of clubs—which he had just drawn from the deck. My previous discard of the 4 of diamonds had enabled him to use his 3 of diamonds in a run, and in effect forced his discard of the 3 of clubs, which he now apparently saw as a safe throw. Actually, it was only "half safe," and was the worst possible discard he could have made. The best discard would have been the 2 or 5 of diamonds. That's right—throw away from the four-card run. Both these cards were dead.

Even if this had been only a three-card spread, I would still throw away from it rather than throw a wild card at this point. Even the King of clubs or the 6 of clubs would have been superior discards. If I were holding three three-card melds, of course this would have allowed me to go gin. But a player who had studied the hand meticulously would realize that this was not likely, based on the cards that had shown; and besides, if I had only one un-matched card I probably would already have knocked. Assuming that I had only two melds in my hand, the King or 6 would add to one of them but would not create a new meld.

The fact that my opponent held onto the King and 6 of clubs reveals that he was playing for an undercut (obviously he could not knock with these cards in his hand) or expected the game to end in a draw by going to the bottom of the deck.

Adding my opponent's 17 unmatched points to the gin bonus of 25, I win 42 points on this hand, plus two extra boxes.

Score at the end of the twelfth hand:

Wander	178
Opponent	87

OFFICIAL GIN RUMMY SCORE PAD
GAME: 200 POINTS

Scoring During Game

After each hand, winner's score is placed in box; each extra box indicated by X in separate box.
Gin: 25 point bonus plus 2 extra boxes.
Undercut: 25 point bonus plus 1 extra box.

Scoring After Game

Game bonus: 200 points.
Winner gets difference between his game score and opponent's.
Each player gets 25 points for each box.
Schneider (loser is scoreless): Double final score.

PLAYER Wander	PLAYER Opponent	PLAYER	PLAYER	PLAYER	PLAYER
13	15				
46	22				
X	57				
X	64				
48	81				
67	87				
136					
X					
X					
178					
X					
X					

Knock Cards

10	5	10	8	9	10	1	2	8	10	2	6					

Post-Game Figuring

Hand Thirteen

My opponent deals, and the knock card is the 10 of spades. My hand is as follows:

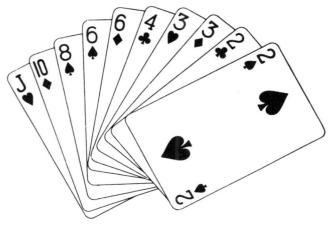

We both refuse the 10 of spades, and I draw the 2 of hearts from the deck. My automatic discard of the 10 of diamonds, however, is taken by my opponent for a diamond run. The 10 of spades, it turns out, has served as a handy fisherman for my opponent just by being there.

My opponent's discard is the Jack of spades. I pick the King of spades from the deck and discard the Jack of hearts. My opponent draws from the deck and knocks with 6 points. I have a net loss of 34.

This kind of game (it lasted for exactly four plays) is, in the vernacular of the gin player, called a "no brainer." It is obvious why the better players prefer longer games so that the factors even off more. Nevertheless, this speedy type of game is not unusual, and it emphasizes the importance of making every play count in every hand.

If my opponent had been playing an average player, quite likely he would have already accumulated as many as 170 points prior to this game during the six hands he had already won. Should that have been true, the 200 point game would have terminated with this no-brainer. As it is, my play has given me a substantial lead where it counts, in points, even though with the hand just completed my opponent has forged ahead 7 to 6 in hands won.

A Two Hundred Point Game

As for the hands that lie ahead, the thing to stamp into your mind is not to permit a "no brainer"—or for that matter, any single occurrence in a game—to throw you off stride or cause carelessness or wildness in your play.

Score at the end of the thirteenth hand:

Wander	178
Opponent	121

Chester Wander
International Gin Rummy Champion

OFFICIAL GIN RUMMY SCORE PAD
GAME: 200 POINTS

Scoring During Game

After each hand, winner's score is placed in box; each extra box indicated by X in separate box.
Gin: 25 point bonus plus 2 extra boxes.
Undercut: 25 point bonus plus 1 extra box.

Scoring After Game

Game bonus: 200 points.
Winner gets difference between his game score and opponent's.
Each player gets 25 points for each box. Schneider (loser is scoreless): Double final score.

PLAYER	PLAYER	PLAYER	PLAYER	PLAYER	PLAYER
Wander	Opponent				
13	15				
46	22				
X	57				
X	64				
48	81				
67	87				
136	121				
X					
X					
178					
X					
X					

Knock Cards

10	5	10	8	9	10	1	2	8	10	2	6	10				

Post-Game Figuring

A Two Hundred Point Game   131

Hand Fourteen

I deal the cards, and the up card is the 6 of clubs. My hand contains the following cards:

My opponent takes the 6 of clubs up card and discards the Jack of hearts. I draw the 4 of diamonds from the deck, which fills in a diamond spread. I discard the King of diamonds, which is protected against a run. Also, it leaves me the flexibility of being able to fill in my diamond spread at either end. Discarding the 10 of diamonds would give me only one way to fill in the diamonds; and besides, it could be used either in an 8-9-10 run or possibly in a spread of three 10s. My Jack of diamonds is, of course, a dead card. However, I see no reason to play it that safe and kill a hand that has a good gin outlook.

My opponent draws the King of hearts from the deck and throws it into the discards. I draw the 8 of diamonds from the deck. I will not release a totally unprotected card like this even though I have an excellent chance to gin. The same, of course, applies to my Ace of hearts, with the added factor that it is a low value card. Yet many an average player would have disposed of the Ace as his first discard of the hand.

Note that I re-evaluate my hand and change my tactics somewhat as this hand progresses.

For my first discard, I chose a safe card over a dead card to keep my hand in a gin setup. Now, however, it narrows to a choice between a dead card and a wild card, and I would rather break up my diamonds than take that risk. I discard the dead Jack of diamonds.

My opponent draws from the deck and throws the 6 of diamonds, which shows me that the 6 of clubs was used in a club run.

I draw the Queen of clubs from the deck, and rather than discard it I decide to release my 10 of diamonds.

My opponent draws from the deck and discards the 6 of hearts from his hand. I draw the 2 of clubs from the deck and discard the Queen of clubs.

My opponent draws from the deck and knocks with 6. I lose a net of 5 points on the hand.

Supposing I had held on relentlessly to my Jack-10 of diamonds, holding out for the 9 or Queen which failed to show up? I would have lost 15 points instead of 5 on my opponent's knock. What's more, if I had thrown him wild cards, he might have been able to knock even sooner and inflict a greater loss on me, or he could have ginned.

Score at the end of the fourteenth hand:

Wander	178
Opponent	126

OFFICIAL GIN RUMMY SCORE PAD
GAME: 200 POINTS

Scoring During Game

After each hand, winner's score is placed in box; each extra box indicated by X in separate box.
Gin: 25 point bonus plus 2 extra boxes.
Undercut: 25 point bonus plus 1 extra box.

Scoring After Game

Game bonus: 200 points.
Winner gets difference between his game score and opponent's.
Each player gets 25 points for each box.
Schneider (loser is scoreless): Double final score.

PLAYER	PLAYER	PLAYER	PLAYER	PLAYER	PLAYER
Wander	Opponent				
13	15				
46	22				
X	57				
X	64				
48	81				
67	87				
136	121				
X	126				
X					
178					
X					
X					

Knock Cards

10	5	10	8	9	10	1	2	8	10	2	6	10	6				

Post-Game Figuring

Hand Fifteen

I deal the cards and turn up the 9 of hearts as the knock card. My hand is the following:

My opponent refuses the up card, and I in turn pass it up. My opponent draws from the deck and discards the King of clubs. I draw the 10 of clubs from the deck and discard the 8 of hearts, which is partially protected by the 9 of hearts. With a meld and other good possibilities already in my hand, I see no reason to make a more defensive play than this.

My opponent draws the 9 of diamonds from the deck and discards it. I draw the Queen of spades from the deck, which gives me three Queens. I discard the 10 of clubs.

My opponent picks from the deck and discards the Queen of hearts, giving me the fourth Queen. I knock with a count of 7. My opponent has the fourth 5, which he lays off on my 5s, and I win 14 points net.

Under less favorable circumstances I might have opened with a safer discard—the Queen of clubs—and would have probably followed it with the Queen of diamonds. The way I played the hand worked out satisfactorily, because a more defensive tack would have cost me the Queen spread. Don't speculate that this is mere good fortune. As I have pointed out before, you have to gear your play to the over-all situation and be prepared for continual changes. In this hand, since my opponent did not pick up any of my discards, there was no reason to digress from the strong play I started out with.

The aim of the expert player is always to stay in control of the game. Not only does he determine his own style of play, but he can utilize his plays to force his opponent into a pattern of play that will work to his benefit. In other words, vigorous play on my part can force my opponent to play strongly also, even though he may not be in as good a position to do so as I am. On the other side of the coin, defensive play by me can force him to slow down even if he is sitting there with beautiful cards.

Score at the end of the fifteenth hand:

| Wander | 192 |
| Opponent | 126 |

OFFICIAL GIN RUMMY SCORE PAD
GAME: 200 POINTS

Scoring During Game

After each hand, winner's score is placed in box; each extra box indicated by X in separate box.
Gin: 25 point bonus plus 2 extra boxes.
Undercut: 25 point bonus plus 1 extra box.

Scoring After Game

Game bonus: 200 points.
Winner gets difference between his game score and opponent's.
Each player gets 25 points for each box.
Schneider (loser is scoreless): Double final score.

PLAYER Wander	PLAYER Opponent	PLAYER	PLAYER	PLAYER	PLAYER
13	15				
46	22				
X	57				
X	64				
48	81				
67	87				
136	121				
X	126				
X					
178					
X					
X					
192					

Knock Cards

10	5	10	8	9	10	1	2	8	10	2	6	10	6	9			

Post-Game Figuring

A Two Hundred Point Game 137

Hand Sixteen

My opponent deals, and the knocking card is the 7 of hearts. My hand is as follows:

We both refuse the 7 of hearts. I pick the 5 of diamonds from the deck. My Queen of spades could be thrown as a fisher. However, even if the play worked by landing me the Queen of clubs, it still would not enable me to knock; and if my opponent picked it up, it might injure my chances of pulling in some of the high cards I could use. This is one of those fairly unusual situations where I visualize a chance to fill in on high cards—and I want to force the game to a fast knock. The discard I select is the 8 of hearts, partially protected by the 7 of hearts knock card.

My opponent draws from the deck and discards the 8 of spades. I draw the Ace of diamonds and now throw the Queen of spades. What has changed since the last play to make this discard a good risk now when it was not before? The new factor is the Ace I have just drawn. Now if my bait hooks the Queen of clubs, I *can* knock, whereas before I would not have been able to. Also, other cards that would give me an immediate knock opportunity are the two 5s that are out.

My opponent picks up the Queen of spades I have just discarded and throws the 5 of spades. I pick up the 5 of spades, turn down my King of clubs, and knock with one point. My opponent has the Jack-Queen-King of spades and the Queen of clubs layoff on my 9-10-Jack of clubs.

Why, you may question, did my opponent not throw his Queen of clubs after my Queen of spades discard? It may be that he recognized my discard as a possible fisher. However, he also had a hand built around high value cards. The difference, of course, was that my spreads were complete in my original hand, whereas he was trying to fill in his combinations.

As a result, he was caught with unmatched high cards at the end of the hand and I won a total of 41 points, ample to give me the game.

Final game score:

Wander	233
Opponent	126

OFFICIAL GIN RUMMY SCORE PAD
GAME: 200 POINTS

Scoring During Game

After each hand, winner's score is placed in box; each extra box indicated by X in separate box.
Gin: 25 point bonus plus 2 extra boxes.
Undercut: 25 point bonus plus 1 extra box.

Scoring After Game

Game bonus: 200 points.
Winner gets difference between his game score and opponent's.
Each player gets 25 points for each box.
Schneider (loser is scoreless): Double final score.

PLAYER	PLAYER	PLAYER	PLAYER	PLAYER	PLAYER
Wander	Opponent				
13	15				
46	22				
X	57				
X	64				
48	81				
67	87				
136	121				
X	126				
X					
178					
X					
X					
192					
233					

Wander, + 457
Opponent, − 457

Knock Cards

10	5	10	8	9	10	1	2	8	10	2	6	10	6	9	7		

Post-Game Figuring

$$\begin{array}{cccc} 233 & 14 & 25 & 200 \\ -126 & -8 & \times 6 & 150 \\ \hline 107 & 6 & 150 & 107 \\ & & & \overline{457} \end{array}$$

Winning at Gin

Post-Game Scoring

The score at the end of the game is 233 for me to 126 for my opponent. We calculate my net total for the game as follows:

I am credited with the difference between my game score and my opponent's:

$$
\begin{array}{r}
233 \\
-126 \\
\hline
107
\end{array}
$$

I am credited with 200 points as a bonus for winning the game.

We count the number of boxes each of us has in the score columns. My opponent has 8 boxes, one for each of the hands he won. I have 14 boxes, 8 of them for the eight hands I won, plus six extra boxes (two each for the three games in which I went gin). The difference between my boxes and my opponent's is figured:

$$
\begin{array}{r}
14 \\
-\ 8 \\
\hline
6
\end{array}
$$

and I am credited with 25 points for each box in excess of my opponent's:

$$
\begin{array}{r}
25 \\
\times 6 \\
\hline
150
\end{array}
$$

My final score for the game is calculated by adding the amounts with which I have been credited:

$$
\begin{array}{r}
107 \\
200 \\
150 \\
\hline
457
\end{array}
$$

General Observations

You will notice that my opponent and I each won an identical number of hands, yet I won nearly twice as many points. Earlier in the book, I mentioned that under normal circumstances I would be able to win a 200 point game by capturing approximately eight hands, whereas an opponent of mine would have to win at least a dozen. Naturally it won't always come out that consistently, but it just so happens this game did, while my opponent's score after winning eight hands was slightly less than two-thirds of the way to a winning total.

This game closely followed the percentages. It was a legitimate contest in which neither player was provided any information regarding the hands of the other. My coming from behind to close the numerical gap and finally win it focuses attention on another point made earlier: that the superiority of the conservative player becomes more noticeable over the long haul.

Had it been a 100 point game, I still would have won it; but at the end of the sixth hand my opponent was only 19 points away from the necessary 100 points, against my modest score of 13. From then on the percentage, based on my carefully calculated play throughout, began to bend in my favor, and following the eleventh hand I took the lead never to be overtaken.

You may have observed that at no time did I pick up a discard of my opponent's for the sole purpose of speculating. With one exception only, I steadfastedly picked up discards to complete a spread. The one exception was a low value turn-up card I accepted that fitted nicely with other low value combinations in my hand and had further merit as a possible knocking card. This pick-up was therefore only partially speculative, since it served a dual purpose.

This does not imply that no situations exist where it is justifiable to speculate. There are isolated cases where it can be a good move, but it should never become a habit for your general method of play. Occasionally you may calculate that a speculative card will be the wedge for a quick knock. Or you may pick one up just to befuddle your opposition, perhaps even to discard it a few plays later. These are very rare and special situations, and this tactic should be discouraged unless you're riding high in the driver's seat and feel you can afford to play bolder than is customary.

Perhaps you have noticed something else in the progression of this game: The five-card spread is something that may be useful in a high knock hand, but it can often prove a disadvantage in a low knock game, because if you end up with a five-card and a three-card meld, that still leaves you with two unmatched cards; and in a low knock game you usually have to rid yourself of all but one unmatched card in order to knock. Five-card melds can be helpful if you are developing a possible second meld at either end of them, which also provides you with safe discards in case the second meld doesn't materialize.

A common mistake made by inexperienced players is to regard a card as untouchable once it becomes part of a meld. Yet several times in the game just concluded a card was thrown from an existing meld (generally it was from a four- or five-card spread, but sometimes it is the correct move even if it breaks up a three-card meld).

By regarding a meld as something sacred on which hangs a mental "Don't Disturb Under Any Circumstances" sign, you are viewing the game too narrowly and losing sight of paramount advantages that a break-up move can sometimes bring you.

The variety of situations that can come up in gin rummy is almost unlimited. This demonstration game covered a wide diversity of plays and playing strategy, but even some fairly common occurrences failed to arise.

As an example, there is one play which an advanced player will sometimes make to avert a layoff. Assume a knock card of 8. The player has just drawn a card and now holds the 5-6-7-8 of diamonds, three 10s, and an unmatched Ace, two deuces, and a 3. Normally he would turn down the 3 and knock with 5 points. Let us say, however, that he knows his opponent has the 9 of diamonds as a layoff. The sophisticated player will turn down the 8 of diamonds, precluding the layoff, and knock with 8 points. Even though he is knocking at a higher level, he has managed to change the 9 of diamonds from an asset to a liability in his opponent's hand and has definitely protected himself against an undercut.

While this game encompassed only a small percentage of the specific situations you will encounter in playing gin rummy, it did embrace most of the basic principles of good play that should be applied to any situation that arises. If you have absorbed these principles, you have taken a giant step toward becoming an expert gin rummy player. If you have the self-discipline to stick to these principles when you play gin rummy tomorrow, or next week, or a month from now, or two years from now—you're eligible to join the ranks of the experts.

Gin rummy is not a game you grow tired of, and this is especially true if you are constantly improving your game. No wonder that for the past twenty-five years gin rummy has been unchallenged in number one place as the most popular card game in the world.

9

What Have You Learned?

Now that you have followed the progress of a complete game of gin rummy, play by play, try your hand at a few specific situations and see how you do. This chapter gives you twelve game situations in which you will come up with the right answer if you apply the gin rummy tactics we've discussed so far. The answers can be found in the second section of the chapter. In order to get the greatest benefit out of this, I urge that you arrive at your own answer before turning the pages to read mine.

The answers are based on following a regular pattern of play. There are times, of course, when you will vary the pattern so that your opponent will not find you too predictable. But such variations should always be careful, logical plays, and not reckless ones.

Don't be dismayed by mistakes. It's one thing to learn a set of principles and quite another to get them working for you. So don't expect to put all your newly acquired knowledge into practice at once.

1. Your opponent has dealt you the following hand:

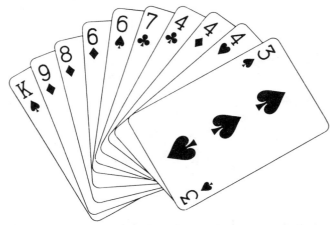

The turn-up card is the King of hearts, which of course you refuse. Your opponent also refuses it. You draw the 2 of diamonds from the deck. What is your discard?

2. Your opponent has dealt you the following hand:

The turn-up card is the 7 of clubs, which you naturally pick up. What is your discard?

Winning at Gin

3. Your opponent has dealt you the following hand:

The up card is the 6 of spades, which both you and your opponent pass up. You pick the 2 of diamonds from the deck. What is your discard?

4. Your opponent has dealt you the following hand:

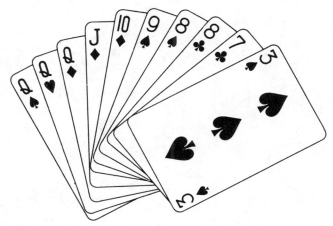

The up card is the 4 of hearts. You refuse it, and your opponent in turn refuses it. You draw the 7 of hearts from the deck. What do you discard?

What Have You Learned?

5. Your opponent has dealt you the following hand:

The up cards is the Ace of clubs. What do you do?

6. Your opponent has dealt you the following hand:

The up card is the 8 of diamonds, which you and your opponent both refuse. You draw the 3 of clubs from the deck. What is your discard?

Winning at Gin

7. The game is in progress. The up card is the Queen of hearts. Each player has had four picks, and neither has picked up any discards of the other. You are holding the following cards:

It is your turn and you draw the 2 of diamonds from the deck. What is your discard?

8. The game is in progress. Your hand is the following:

The up card is the 5 of hearts. Each player has had half a dozen turns. Your opponent has picked the 9 of spades from the discards. Your opponent has just discarded the 2 of hearts, and it is now your turn. What do you do?

What Have You Learned? 149

9. The game is in progress. The up card is the 10 of diamonds. Earlier in the hand you picked the King of clubs from the discard pile. Your opponent picked the 7 of hearts from the discard pile. Each player has had five picks. Your hand is as follows:

It is your pick. You draw the Ace of spades from the deck. What is your play?

10. The game is in progress. The knock card was the 10 of hearts (which you took). Your hand reads as follows:

Each player has had ten picks. Your opponent has taken the following cards from the discard pile during the hand: Jack of spades, 8 of hearts, 6 of diamonds. It is your turn and you draw the 4 of spades from the deck. What is your play?

11. The hand has progressed to the point where it is your pick from the deck, and you are drawing the fiftieth card. The knock is 4. During the course of the hand, your opponent has picked the King of clubs, the 2 of diamonds, and the 7 of clubs from the discard pile. Queens have been discarded by each player earlier in the hand. Your hand is as follows:

The card that you pick from the deck is the 8 of clubs. What do you do now?

12. The turn-up card is the Ace of diamonds—you are playing this hand for gin. Your hand is as follows, after the hand has gone halfway down the deck:

Kings have been discarded by both players. You draw the 9 of diamonds from the deck. What is your discard?

Answers

1. Your discard is the King of spades. To back up for a moment, did you question my automatic refusal of the King of hearts knock card? Some novice players might pick it up to go with the King of spades, discarding the useless—but absolutely wild—7 of clubs, hoping it will serve as bait for the 7 of diamonds. There is no justification whatsoever for such a play. This is pure speculation, and in the highest value cards at that.

The King of spades is protected against being used for three Kings, since your opponent has refused the King of hearts. The only way it could be used would be in a King-Queen-Jack run. Therefore it is the best protected card in your hand and also rids you of a high value card.

2. Your discard is the 5 of hearts. Your 5 of clubs is employed in a meld, and of course provides protection for the 5 of hearts. A too defensive player would throw the 10 of hearts because it is of no use to the hand presently and is a higher value card. However, it is totally unprotected at this point, and until you see how the hand develops it is a much poorer choice than the 5 of hearts.

3. Your discard is the 7 of spades. Were you tempted to pick up the 6 of spades? I hope not. It should become automatic with you to reject such a card under these circumstances. Not only is it speculative but there is a distinct advantage to you in leaving it on the table, since it becomes an automatic fisherman for the 6 of diamonds. Not only that, If you picked it up, you would put your opponent on guard against discarding any cards that might fit around it—including the 6 of diamonds which you could use so handily.

You have protection for the 7 of spades from several directions: the 7 of diamonds in your hand, the 6 of spades on the table, and the 10-Jack of spades in your hand. If your opponent should pick it up, he would be limited to a three-card meld and you have layoffs on any meld he could make with it.

4. Your discard is the Queen of spades. In this hand there is only one totally unprotected card: the 3 of spades. Yet a surprising number of players would rashly get rid of it as a "misfit" in the

hand, giving no thought to the fact that, in terms of percentage, it's the card in the hand most likely to be grabbed up by their opponent.

Since the Queen of diamonds is tied up in a run, the two remaining Queens are nicely protected cards. The Queen of spades has an added advantage as a discard because your 9-8 of spades help block a run at one end. The Queen of hearts would be second choice as a discard.

Do you see why it is better to hold the Queen-Jack-10 of diamonds instead of keeping the three Queens intact? You can add to the Queen-Jack-10 combination at either end, whereas there is only one card in the deck, the fourth Queen, that could be added to a Queen meld. What's more, the 10 and Jack of diamonds are wilder discards than the Queens.

Or are you asking, why break up the handsome setup at all? Why not give it a whirl for a play or two, and maybe end up with Queens *and* the Queen-Jack-10? You have a hand with several other very attractive meld possibilities. There are only two cards that would give you two melds out of your high cards: the Queen of clubs and the 9 of diamonds. It is absolutely wrong to wait around for those cards. What's more, playing the hand this way keeps you more flexible by giving you a chance to fill in your hand in other areas where a greater number of possibilities exist.

5. Your play is the following: (a) You pick up the Ace of clubs up card. This is one of those rare instances where it is wise to pick up a turned-up card that does not immediately complete a meld. There are several reasons for this. First of all, you have a poor hand and you must start the play defensively. Secondly, the Ace of course is a very low card and also matches cards in your hand for possible melds. Also, this move will prevent your opponent from taking the card, which is a distinct probability, since under these conditions cards of low value like this are fair game for a good player. Your object at this point should be to convert an unpromising hand into a playable hand, at the same time keeping your unmatched cards at a low level.

(b) You discard the 9 of clubs. The 9 of clubs is a protected card, and at the same time reduces your unmatched point count by 8 points when you trade it for the Ace of clubs. In the next two plays—depending, of course, on what develops—the most probable discards would be the 9 of hearts and the Jack of hearts, in that order.

In continuing the play of this hand, the next three picks turned up some very usable cards in the 4-5-6 range, changing the hand from a poor one to a strong one with good winning possibilities.

6. Your discard is the Queen of spades. This card is all but dead—the chance of its being used for Queens is slight, and in that case you would have a layoff. It is a better protected card than the Queen of hearts, which would be the next logical discard.

Did you come to this conclusion, or did you have your eye on the 7 of diamonds as a discard because the 8 of diamonds on the table and the 7 of spades in your hand seemed to give it solid protection? This protection is not so solid as it looks. The 7 of diamonds can still be used to make three 7s or a 7-6-5 run. Additionally, the Queens rid you of higher value cards. After you have discarded both Queens—and assuming that your hand has not filled in around your 7s—then the 7 of diamonds might come under consideration as a discard.

7. Your discard is the 4 of spades—face down! In other words, you *knock* with 10 points. Those unmatched cards look awfully easy to fill in, don't they? Forget it. The game is young—you have a chance to knock—do it.

8. You pick up the 2 of hearts, place it with your 2 of spades and Ace of spades—then turn your 3 of clubs face down on the discard pile and knock with 5 points.

9. Your play is to turn down a 5 and knock with 10 points.

Are you getting the message? This is a point I have probably made more often than any other in this book. When you are in a position to knock—unless there are extenuating circumstances, which is rare—KNOCK.

10. You discard the 4 of spades and continue to play. Obviously, you could knock at this point by throwing the 5 of clubs. However, it is also obvious that your opponent, based on the discards he has picked up, has three melds and is playing for gin. The hand has progressed to within a few cards of the bottom of the deck. If you knock, it is certain that you will be undercut.

Winning at Gin

The cards your opponent has picked up indicate he would have no use for the 4 of spades. It acts as a perfect fisherman for you to bait the 4 of clubs, which would give you gin.

Just one note here: The conclusions drawn above about the opponent's hand are based on the assumption that he is a capable player who is making logical plays. If he is a reckless player who speculates wildly, you would of course play your own hand accordingly and would have a much easier time beating him than if he played properly.

11. You discard the Queen of clubs. That should end the hand in a draw.

By turning down the 4 of clubs, you could knock with 3 points; but the chances are that you would be undercut. Your opponent had picked the 7 of clubs, and the 5-6 of clubs have not appeared in the discards. The logical assumption is that these three cards constitute one of his melds. He has picked up the 2 of diamonds, and the 3-4 of diamonds have not shown. Presumably he has a low diamond run. His third meld obviously is Kings.

Since he is sitting with three melds in his hand, your opponent is surely in a position to knock, but—like you—he has held back for fear of being undercut. At this late point in the hand, the danger is that you will become lax and make one of two mistakes: knock—or throw your opponent a card which will enable him to go gin.

12. Your discard is the King of diamonds. Why break away from a meld? First of all, the King of diamonds is a dead card. Secondly, in a hand that is committed to gin, the chances are very remote that a five-card run will do your hand any good. Your two-two-three combination offers four opportunities to fill in as a meld. There is no reason in the world to break away from it at this point. Later in the hand that might be correct to do, but at this juncture the King of diamonds is the safest and most logical discard.

What Have You Learned?

10
A Final Word

Do you feel prepared now to return to the gin rummy wars, well armed and ready for battle? If you've been able to absorb everything written here, I can promise you some pleasant surprises when you go back to the game table.

For some of you, if you are already very experienced gin rummy players, the contents of this book may result in modifications in your game. For others the effect may be much more radical: it may mean doing a lot of things exactly the *opposite* of the way you've been doing them through many years of "playing at" gin rummy. If you're a novice, you're particularly dear to my heart—you are in a unique position to learn the game correctly from the beginning. If you apply the lessons you've learned, you have every chance of moving quickly up to the expert class.

Whichever category you belong to, what follows is important to you. This is a review of my basic guides to good gin rummy playing. You should commit these guides to memory. Until you do, read them over from time to time. They will serve as a refresher on what to keep in mind when you're playing the game.

The guides listed below are a nutshell condensation of the points I have been making. Earlier in the book I have explained the reasons for them, illustrated how they work in actual practice in the course of a game, and tested your ability to apply them in the series of questions posed in the previous chapter.

156

Now, for your handy reference, here they are in summary form: my sixteen basic principles of good play.

1. Study your opponent. Observe his style of play, how he sets his cards in his hand, his pattern of throwing discards, how much he speculates. Be confident but not overconfident, and never underestimate your opponent.

2. When the deal has been completed, always count your cards to make sure there has not been a misdeal.

3. At the beginning of each hand, check the game score and note carefully the knocking card. These are two important factors in determining how you should play the hand.

4. Keep your opponent off guard by varying your pattern of play and rearranging your hand from time to time, and avoid any mannerisms that will give your opponent valuable tips about your own play.

5. As a general practice, don't speculate by picking up discards that will not complete a meld in your hand.

6. Never discard a card you have just picked up until you have placed it in your hand and shifted your cards around.

7. Don't be afraid to discard an add-on card to a meld your opponent is holding if it is the logical play to make at the moment.

8. Don't be afraid to break up meld possibilities—or even melds—if it will assure you of safe discards or if it will otherwise serve your interests. This is especially true when the combinations you break are of high face value, since you may at the same time be able to build your hand along more favorable lines.

9. Avoid getting caught with a blocked hand—that is, a hand built around melds that are blocked at one or both ends, which give you little or no chance of knocking or going gin.

10. Never forget the importance of layoffs, which often can enable you to undercut your opponent. Proper play can provide you with layoffs you may not even be aware of.

11. Pay close attention to the cards that are discarded; your ability to remember them can mean the difference between winning and losing.

12. With few exceptions, always knock at the first opportunity.

13. In a gin hand, don't be afraid to break away from a meld if necessary in order to avoid a risky play that could give your opponent gin.

14. Don't gamble on reckless plays simply because you are near the bottom of the deck. It may be wiser to try for a draw rather than make a rash move and throw the hand.

15. Always look at your opponent's hand when it is laid down to make sure it is as called.

16. Finally—and emphatically—*play percentages*. Reckless play can cost you not only the hand but the game.

If I were asked to reduce my philosophy of gin rummy playing to one word, I wouldn't hesitate a moment before giving my answer: THINK. That's the basic ingredient of every one of the guiding principles I have just given you. That's the common denominator of everything this book is about. THINK. Then when you encounter variations of things you've read here in actual play, you'll know *which* principles to apply and *how* to apply them.

In the beginning, you may find that putting your newly acquired knowledge into practice under actual playing conditions is a challenge not easily met. There will be instances when you will be beset by confusion and uncertainties, as you try to apply everything you've learned at once. Don't be discouraged. You are bound to make mistakes. But beyond any doubt, and more rapidly than you probably expect, your play will show marked improvement.

Now—while I urge you always to keep the above firmly in mind—let me add a tempering word. Don't be afraid to play more slowly than has been your custom; but on the other hand don't reduce the pace to that of a chess game, where ten minutes or more is considered quite a respectable interval between moves. If you try to figure out every possible consequence of every single play you might make, you're apt to find yourself getting completely bogged down. Not only would this make you unpopular with your opponents, but—more important—it might backfire by ruining your own continuity of thought and giving you the jitters. Also, an indecisive and tedious style of play probably would kill the atmosphere of enjoyment that should surround any good gin rummy game.

If you follow my advice to the letter and figure every move scientifically, you may tend to be somewhat overcautious to start with. Don't worry. Later, as you become more skillful, many of your responses will become automatic reflexes, triggered by the information and experience previously fed into the built-in computer called your brain.

And the game is a pleasure to play!

Illustrative of the card player who overly figures each move is a story credited to a close friend of mine, Charles Barton, director of Abbott & Costello films and such TV shows as Amos 'n Andy and Dennis the Menace.

It concerns a studious horse player—the breed that buys the racing form the minute it hits the stands. It is his bible. He rushes home with it and pores over it, figuring every race, handicapping every entry from every possible angle.

Like many horse players, although he knows well in advance which horse he is going to bet on, this fellow waits until the two-minute buzzer sounds before rushing to a window and getting his wager down.

One day at Santa Anita he sits next to a happy-go-lucky player who is drinking beer, talking up a storm, and enjoying himself to the fullest. Happy Boy has no racing form or tip sheets and hardly bothers even to glance at his program. He is also a member of the two-minute buzzer school of bettors, always weaving his way to the window just before it closes.

The first race is run, and Happy Boy whoops with joy—he has a winner. The meticulous handicapper is out of the money and is chagrined.

When the second race is over, Happy Boy once again holds a winning ticket. The careful handicapper comes up empty.

The same thing happens in the third race. By now the handicapper is overcome with frustration. He can't contain himself any longer. Turning to his money-waving neighbor, he asks:

"How in the world do you do it? Here I've got a scientific approach to figuring each race, and I lose. I can't see you doing anything to make intelligent selections—yet you've tabbed three winners in a row. What's your system?"

Happy Boy explains good-naturedly, "The trouble with you is that you do *too much* figuring."

"But how do you pick your horses?"

Offering his newfound friend a beer, Happy Boy explains: "Well, in the first race, when the buzzer sounded I dropped my cigarette and it fell on the program on No. 2, so I bet the No. 2 horse and it won. In the second race, I happened to look up when the buzzer sounded and there were three birds flying by. So I bet horse No. 3—and it won. Then in the third race, I just added 2 and 3 and bet on horse No. 7."

"But," protests the handicapper, "2 and 3 don't add up to 7. They total 5."

"See," says Happy Boy, "there you go with your darned figuring again."

A lesson can be learned from this story that is applicable to gin rummy. In capsule form it is: DON'T GO OVERBOARD.

Study this book. Read it twice if necessary. Apply what you can remember the next time you sit down to a game. Each succeeding time you play, your growing flexibility, discipline, and ability to play shifting patterns will make you more expert.

—And some day I may meet you in the International Gin Rummy Tournament at Las Vegas.

MELVIN POWERS SELF-IMPROVEMENT LIBRARY

ASTROLOGY

___ASTROLOGY—HOW TO CHART YOUR HOROSCOPE Max Heindel 7.00
___ASTROLOGY AND SEXUAL ANALYSIS Morris C. Goodman 10.00
___ASTROLOGY AND YOU Carroll Righter 5.00
___ASTROLOGY MADE EASY Astarte 7.00
___ASTROLOGY, ROMANCE, YOU AND THE STARS Anthony Norvell 10.00
___MY WORLD OF ASTROLOGY Sydney Omarr 10.00
___THOUGHT DIAL Sydney Omarr 7.00
___WHAT THE STARS REVEAL ABOUT THE MEN IN YOUR LIFE Thelma White 3.00

BRIDGE

___BRIDGE BIDDING MADE EASY Edwin B. Kantar 15.00
___BRIDGE CONVENTIONS Edwin B. Kantar 10.00
___COMPETITIVE BIDDING IN MODERN BRIDGE Edgar Kaplan 7.00
___DEFENSIVE BRIDGE PLAY COMPLETE Edwin B Kantar 20.00
___GAMESMAN BRIDGE—PLAY BETTER WITH KANTAR Edwin B. Kantar 7.00
___HOW TO IMPROVE YOUR BRIDGE Alfred Sheinwold 7.00
___IMPROVING YOUR BIDDING SKILLS Edwin B. Kantar 10.00
___INTRODUCTION TO DECLARER'S PLAY Edwin B. Kantar 7.00
___INTRODUCTION TO DEFENDER'S PLAY Edwin B. Kantar 10.00
___KANTAR FOR THE DEFENSE Edwin B. Kantar 10.00
___KANTAR FOR THE DEFENSE VOLUME 2 Edwin B. Kantar 10.00
___TEST YOUR BRIDGE PLAY Edwin B. Kantar 10.00
___VOLUME 2—TEST YOUR BRIDGE PLAY Edwin B. Kantar 10.00
___WINNING DECLARER PLAY Dorothy Hayden Truscott 10.00

BUSINESS, STUDY & REFERENCE

___BRAINSTORMING Charles Clark 10.00
___CONVERSATION MADE EASY Elliot Russell 5.00
___EXAM SECRET Dennis B. Jackson 7.00
___FIX-IT BOOK Arthur Symons 2.00
___HOW TO DEVELOP A BETTER SPEAKING VOICE M. Hellier 5.00
___HOW TO SAVE 50% ON GAS & CAR EXPENSES Ken Stansbie 5.00
___HOW TO SELF-PUBLISH YOUR BOOK & MAKE IT A BEST SELLER Melvin Powers . . 20.00
___INCREASE YOUR LEARNING POWER Geoffrey A. Dudley 5.00
___PRACTICAL GUIDE TO BETTER CONCENTRATION Melvin Powers 5.00
___PUBLIC SPEAKING MADE EASY Thomas Montalbo 10.00
___7 DAYS TO FASTER READING William S. Schaill 7.00
___SONGWRITER'S RHYMING DICTIONARY Jane Shaw Whitfield 10.00
___SPELLING MADE EASY Lester D. Basch & Dr. Milton Finkelstein 3.00
___STUDENT'S GUIDE TO BETTER GRADES J.A. Rickard 3.00
___TEST YOURSELF—FIND YOUR HIDDEN TALENT Jack Shafer 3.00
___YOUR WILL & WHAT TO DO ABOUT IT Attorney Samuel G. King 7.00

CALLIGRAPHY

___ADVANCED CALLIGRAPHY Katherine Jeffares 7.00
___CALLIGRAPHY—THE ART OF BEAUTIFUL WRITING Katherine Jeffares 7.00
___CALLIGRAPHY FOR FUN & PROFIT Anne Leptich & Jacque Evans 10.00
___CALLIGRAPHY MADE EASY Tina Serafini 7.00

CHESS & CHECKERS

___BEGINNER'S GUIDE TO WINNING CHESS Fred Reinfeld 10.00
___CHESS IN TEN EASY LESSONS Larry Evans 10.00
___CHESS MADE EASY Milton L. Hanauer 5.00
___CHESS PROBLEMS FOR BEGINNERS Edited by Fred Reinfeld 7.00

_____ CHESS TACTICS FOR BEGINNERS Edited by Fred Reinfeld 7.00
_____ HOW TO WIN AT CHECKERS Fred Reinfeld 7.00
_____ 1001 BRILLIANT WAYS TO CHECKMATE Fred Reinfeld 10.00
_____ 1001 WINNING CHESS SACRIFICES & COMBINATIONS Fred Reinfeld 10.00

COOKERY & HERBS
_____ CULPEPER'S HERBAL REMEDIES Dr. Nicholas Culpeper 5.00
_____ FAST GOURMET COOKBOOK Poppy Cannon 2.50
_____ HEALING POWER OF HERBS May Bethel 5.00
_____ HEALING POWER OF NATURAL FOODS May Bethel 7.00
_____ HERBS FOR HEALTH—HOW TO GROW & USE THEM Louise Evans Doole 7.00
_____ HOME GARDEN COOKBOOK—DELICIOUS NATURAL FOOD RECIPES Ken Kraft 3.00
_____ MEATLESS MEAL GUIDE Tomi Ryan & James H. Ryan, M.D. 4.00
_____ VEGETABLE GARDENING FOR BEGINNERS Hugh Wilberg 2.00
_____ VEGETABLES FOR TODAY'S GARDENS R. Milton Carleton 2.00
_____ VEGETARIAN COOKERY Janet Walker 10.00
_____ VEGETARIAN COOKING MADE EASY & DELECTABLE Veronica Vezza 3.00

GAMBLING & POKER
_____ HOW TO WIN AT POKER Terence Reese & Anthony T. Watkins 10.00
_____ SCARNE ON DICE John Scarne 15.00
_____ WINNING AT CRAPS Dr. Lloyd T. Commins 10.00
_____ WINNING AT GIN Chester Wander & Cy Rice 10.00
_____ WINNING AT POKER—AN EXPERT'S GUIDE John Archer 10.00
_____ WINNING AT 21—AN EXPERT'S GUIDE John Archer 10.00
_____ WINNING POKER SYSTEMS Norman Zadeh 10.00

HEALTH
_____ BEE POLLEN Lynda Lyngheim & Jack Scagnetti 5.00
_____ COPING WITH ALZHEIMER'S Rose Oliver, Ph.D. & Francis Bock, Ph.D. 10.00
_____ DR. LINDNER'S POINT SYSTEM FOOD PROGRAM Peter G Lindner, M.D. 2.00
_____ HELP YOURSELF TO BETTER SIGHT Margaret Darst Corbett 7.00
_____ HOW YOU CAN STOP SMOKING PERMANENTLY Ernest Caldwell 5.00
_____ MIND OVER PLATTER Peter G Lindner, M.D. 5.00
_____ NATURE'S WAY TO NUTRITION & VIBRANT HEALTH Robert J. Scrutton 3.00
_____ NEW CARBOHYDRATE DIET COUNTER Patti Lopez-Pereira 2.00
_____ REFLEXOLOGY Dr. Maybelle Segal 7.00
_____ REFLEXOLOGY FOR GOOD HEALTH Anna Kaye & Don C. Matchan 10.00
_____ 30 DAYS TO BEAUTIFUL LEGS Dr. Marc Selner 3.00
_____ WONDER WITHIN Thomas S. Coyle, M.D. 10.00
_____ YOU CAN LEARN TO RELAX Dr. Samuel Gutwirth 5.00

HYPNOTISM
_____ CHILDBIRTH WITH HYPNOSIS William S. Kroger, M.D. 5.00
_____ HOW TO SOLVE YOUR SEX PROBLEMS WITH SELF-HYPNOSIS Frank Caprio, M.D. ... 5.00
_____ HOW YOU CAN BOWL BETTER USING SELF-HYPNOSIS Jack Heise 7.00
_____ HOW YOU CAN PLAY BETTER GOLF USING SELF-HYPNOSIS Jack Heise 3.00
_____ HYPNOSIS AND SELF-HYPNOSIS Bernard Hollander, M.D. 7.00
_____ HYPNOTISM (Originally published 1893) Carl Sextus 5.00
_____ HYPNOTISM MADE EASY Dr. Ralph Winn 10.00
_____ HYPNOTISM MADE PRACTICAL Louis Orton 5.00
_____ MODERN HYPNOSIS Lesley Kuhn & Salvatore Russo, Ph.D. 5.00
_____ NEW CONCEPTS OF HYPNOSIS Bernard C. Gindes, M.D. 10.00
_____ NEW SELF-HYPNOSIS Paul Adams 10.00
_____ POST-HYPNOTIC INSTRUCTIONS—SUGGESTIONS FOR THERAPY Arnold Furst ... 10.00
_____ PRACTICAL GUIDE TO SELF-HYPNOSIS Melvin Powers 10.00
_____ PRACTICAL HYPNOTISM Philip Magonet, M.D. 3.00
_____ SECRETS OF HYPNOTISM S.J. Van Pelt, M.D. 5.00
_____ SELF-HYPNOSIS—A CONDITIONED-RESPONSE TECHNIQUE Laurence Sparks 7.00

_____ SELF-HYPNOSIS—ITS THEORY, TECHNIQUE & APPLICATION Melvin Powers 7.00
_____ THERAPY THROUGH HYPNOSIS Edited by Raphael H. Rhodes 5.00

JUST FOR WOMEN

_____ COSMOPOLITAN'S GUIDE TO MARVELOUS MEN Foreword by Helen Gurley Brown .. 3.00
_____ COSMOPOLITAN'S HANG-UP HANDBOOK Foreword by Helen Gurley Brown 4.00
_____ COSMOPOLITAN'S LOVE BOOK—A GUIDE TO ECSTASY IN BED 7.00
_____ COSMOPOLITAN'S NEW ETIQUETTE GUIDE Foreword by Helen Gurley Brown 4.00
_____ I AM A COMPLEAT WOMAN Doris Hagopian & Karen O'Connor Sweeney 3.00
_____ JUST FOR WOMEN—A GUIDE TO THE FEMALE BODY Richard E. Sand M.D. 5.00
_____ NEW APPROACHES TO SEX IN MARRIAGE John E. Eichenlaub, M.D. 3.00
_____ SEXUALLY ADEQUATE FEMALE Frank S. Caprio, M.D. 3.00
_____ SEXUALLY FULFILLED WOMAN Dr. Rachel Copelan 5.00

MARRIAGE, SEX & PARENTHOOD

_____ ABILITY TO LOVE Dr. Allan Fromme 7.00
_____ GUIDE TO SUCCESSFUL MARRIAGE Drs. Albert Ellis & Robert Harper 10.00
_____ HOW TO RAISE AN EMOTIONALLY HEALTHY, HAPPY CHILD Albert Ellis, Ph.D. 10.00
_____ PARENT SURVIVAL TRAINING Marvin Silverman, Ed.D. & David Lustig, Ph.D. 10.00
_____ POTENCY MIRACLE Uri P. Peles, M.D. 10.00
_____ SEX WITHOUT GUILT Albert Ellis, Ph.D. 7.00
_____ SEXUALLY ADEQUATE MALE Frank S. Caprio, M.D. 3.00
_____ SEXUALLY FULFILLED MAN Dr. Rachel Copelan 5.00
_____ STAYING IN LOVE Dr. Norton F. Kristy 7.00

MELVIN POWERS MAIL ORDER LIBRARY

_____ HOW TO GET RICH IN MAIL ORDER Melvin Powers 20.00
_____ HOW TO SELF-PUBLISH YOUR BOOK Melvin Powers 20.00
_____ HOW TO WRITE A GOOD ADVERTISEMENT Victor O. Schwab 20.00
_____ MAIL ORDER MADE EASY J. Frank Brumbaugh 20.00
_____ MAKING MONEY WITH CLASSIFIED ADS Melvin Powers 20.00

METAPHYSICS & OCCULT

_____ CONCENTRATION—A GUIDE TO MENTAL MASTERY Mouni Sadhu 10.00
_____ EXTRA-TERRESTRIAL INTELLIGENCE—THE FIRST ENCOUNTER 6.00
_____ FORTUNE TELLING WITH CARDS P. Foli 10.00
_____ HOW TO INTERPRET DREAMS, OMENS & FORTUNE TELLING SIGNS Gettings 5.00
_____ HOW TO UNDERSTAND YOUR DREAMS Geoffrey A. Dudley 7.00
_____ MAGICIAN—HIS TRAINING AND WORK W.E. Butler 7.00
_____ MEDITATION Mouni Sadhu 10.00
_____ MODERN NUMEROLOGY Morris C. Goodman 5.00
_____ NUMEROLOGY—ITS FACTS AND SECRETS Ariel Yvon Taylor 5.00
_____ NUMEROLOGY MADE EASY W. Mykian 5.00
_____ PALMISTRY MADE EASY Fred Gettings 7.00
_____ PALMISTRY MADE PRACTICAL Elizabeth Daniels Squire 7.00
_____ PROPHECY IN OUR TIME Martin Ebon 2.50
_____ SUPERSTITION—ARE YOU SUPERSTITIOUS? Eric Maple 2.00
_____ TAROT OF THE BOHEMIANS Papus 10.00
_____ WAYS TO SELF-REALIZATION Mouni Sadhu 7.00
_____ WITCHCRAFT, MAGIC & OCCULTISM—A FASCINATING HISTORY W.B. Crow 10.00
_____ WITCHCRAFT—THE SIXTH SENSE Justine Glass 7.00

RECOVERY

_____ KNIGHT IN RUSTY ARMOR Robert Fisher 5.00
_____ KNIGHT IN RUSTY ARMOR (Hard cover edition) Robert Fisher 10.00
_____ KNIGHTS WITHOUT ARMOR (Hard cover edition) Aaron R. Kipnis, Ph.D. 10.00
_____ PRINCESS WHO BELIEVED IN FAIRY TALES Marcia Grad 10.00

SELF-HELP & INSPIRATIONAL

Available from your bookstore or directly from Melvin Powers.
Please add $2.00 shipping and handling for each book ordered.

Melvin Powers

12015 Sherman Road, No. Hollywood, California 91605

For our complete catalog, visit our Web site at http://www.mpowers.com.